BE THE
Change

"Never doubt that a small group of thoughtful, committed citizens can change the world. Indeed, it is the only thing that ever has."

—*Margaret Mead*

BE *The* *Change*

HOW TO GET WHAT YOU WANT IN **YOUR** COMMUNITY

Thomas Linzey with Anneke Campbell

GIBBS SMITH
TO ENRICH AND INSPIRE HUMANKIND
Salt Lake City | Charleston | Santa Fe | Santa Barbara

To Stacey, Richard, Ben, Gail, Shireen, Ellen, Steve, Michael,
Mari, Shannon, Kai, and Chad—the ones who went first; to
all of the municipal officials who have taken the plunge with
them; and to the woods, where this great adventure began.

First Edition
13 12 11 10 09   5 4 3 2 1

Text © 2009 Anneke Campbell

Published by
Gibbs Smith
P.O. Box 667
Layton, Utah 84041

1.800.835.4993 orders
www.gibbs-smith.com

Cover design by Black Eye Design
Interior design and production by Jocelyn Foye
Printed and bound in Canada
Gibbs Smith books are printed on either recycled, 100% post-consumer waste, FSC-certified papers or on paper produced from a 100% certified sustainable forest/controlled wood source.

Library of Congress Cataloging-in-Publication Data

Linzey, Thomas.
  Be the change : how to get what you want in your community /
Thomas Linzey with Anneke Campbell. — 1st ed.
    p. cm.
  ISBN-13: 978-1-4236-0561-4
  ISBN-10: 1-4236-0561-6
  1. Community organization. I. Campbell, Anneke. II. Title.
  HM766.L56 2009
  303.4—dc22
                        2009006211

CONTENTS

I n the pages that follow, you will meet people from all walks of life who have left their comfort zones to become community leaders.

You will meet Gail Darrell from New Hampshire, who left gardening to stop water-withdrawal corporations from taking her town's water, and Michael Vacca, from western Pennsylvania, who pours concrete by day and tries to stop coal corporations from destroying his community by night. You will meet Cathy Miorelli, a local elected official and nurse who, at a diminutive five feet, has fearlessly led her borough council in taking on some of the largest waste corporations in the state of Pennsylvania. And you will meet Rick Evans, a Spokane, Washington, member of the Laborers Union, who is working with others to protect the constitutional rights of workers.

If you met these people on the street, you wouldn't think twice about them. But if you were to meet them in city hall, in a town meeting, or in a public hearing, you would watch them transform into fighters for their community and advocates for local self-government. These people know that they have the inalienable right to alter, reform, or abolish their government in order to achieve a better, stronger community. And they're willing to devote their lives to making it happen.

It's been a great pleasure over the past ten years to work with these people. All have become colleagues, and many have become close friends. None of them waited for someone to give them permission to act in defense of their communities. They didn't wait for an environmental group to come along and try to save them, or for a state or federal agency to intervene. Just as important, they refused to listen to anyone who told them there was nothing they could do to keep their communities from being damaged or destroyed.

They just did it. They did it because they had run out of hope that anyone else would.

And so they stood up and began reprogramming their local governments. They demanded that their elected officials find a new way to protect the rights of residents. In so doing, they have transformed the members of their local governments from mere administrators into the lead wave of a movement toward sustainability through local self-governance.

That, of course, sounds complicated. But the people laying the groundwork for a broader movement would tell you that they're just bringing their local governments in line with the principles laid out in the Declaration of Independence. And the one principle from the Declaration that has been driven into every single state constitution is this: governments exist primarily to protect the rights of people and communities, and when they stop doing so, they must be changed or abolished.

Giving up hope that someone else will do this for them has freed them to do whatever they need to do—which includes slamming themselves up against 140 years of well-settled law.

Giving up hope has liberated them to take whatever steps they need to take—declaring that ecosystems have rights that need to be defended within their communities, forcing their local elected officials to resign when they refuse to do the will of community majorities, and getting sued for challenging court proclamations which claim that corporations have more rights than the communities in which they do business.

It's structural change they're after, because they've become convinced that nothing short of this will actually take their communities off the defensive and put them in a place where they control their own futures. In short, they do it because there's nothing left to lose anymore in their communities. The cost of doing nothing now outweighs the cost of acting.

You may be surprised to learn that most of the people who appear in the pages ahead don't know each other. That will be changing in the years to come, as community leaders across the country join hands to begin a journey that will end with new local and state constitutions, and perhaps even the rewriting of the United States Constitution. These people are convinced—from the things they've seen, heard, and experienced—that nothing short of a complete overhaul will solve the problems they face in their communities. And the results of their battles will eventually determine the course of a much larger challenge: whether we will continue to allow others to destroy our communities and the planet, or whether we will somehow find a way to align our governance and law with sustainable living.

So as you head into the pages that follow, we hope that you go beyond merely cheering for these folks who have pioneered a different kind of activism. They are relying on you to help them by doing the same in your community.

In the end, you'll hear them saying something quite simple: it's time to give up on the hope that others will help you. Get on with doing the work that will save the communities and places that you love. In taking action, you will become part of a group that, when joined with others, will create a movement that will be impossible to stop.

—Thomas Linzey

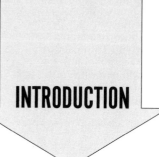

INTRODUCTION

Thomas Linzey and the Democracy School

Three thousand environmental activists have gathered together for the annual Bioneers conference in San Rafael, California. It's a pantheon of environmental movers and shakers: rain forest protectors, GMO opponents, the elite of green designers and green tech innovators, as well as indigenous leaders and social justice advocates, all gathering to gain the inspiration and energy to wage the good fight for another year. But who is this guy standing at the podium in a suit and tie who looks like a Republican bubba? Who has even heard of the Community Environmental Legal Defense Fund? Two minutes into his speech, the crowd is riveted. When he declares that "the only thing environmental regulation regulates is environmentalists," his audience cheers in recognition. When he quietly states, "There has never been an environmental movement in America because movements drive rights into the Constitution, and rivers and cougars and ecosystems have no rights," people in the crowd rise up, stamping their feet.

This affirmation bespeaks the frustration of activists who have watched as federal laws such as the Clean Air and Clean Water acts, and similar state laws, have actually *legalized* environmental harms by shifting focus away from the harms themselves to regulating how much pollution or destruction of nature is allowed. Once an activity is declared legal by federal or state governments, local governments are prohibited from banning that activity, no matter what the future damage. Many of these same activists are unaware of the common cause at the root of their specific problem, which consists of a complex layering of law that keeps communities from exercising their right to say no. It's as if the abolitionists tried to regulate the number of whiplashes that could be used on every separate plantation but never declared the practice of slavery itself illegal.

As a member of Thomas Linzey's audience, I was curious to understand how this inspirational speaker came to pioneer a whole new way of looking at the law. We initiated a conversation, which eventually led to the writing of this book.

Thomas Linzey grew up in Mobile, Alabama, surrounded by animals. Big tortoises crept underfoot and flying squirrels bounded overhead. His family raised baby raccoons and nursed back to health a blue jay, which liked to perch on his shoulder during breakfast. A flamingo, blown in by a storm, stalked the front yard, a living lawn ornament. Today his parents might be called "wildlife rehabilitators," but at the time, he assumed everybody lived this way.

As a first-year law student at Widener Law School in Pennsylvania, Linzey persuaded a former lawyer for the Environmental Protection Agency to take him on as a research assistant. He dug into law review articles, investigating corporate charters in relation to pollution. He found that all fifty states have statutes in place, most from the 1800s, which allow a state's attorney general to revoke a corporate charter in the event of wrongdoing. These statutes, however, have rarely been used for anything substantive. He wrote an article arguing that this power of revocation could be wielded by citizens in order to hold corporations directly responsible for the damage they create. "I did this work," he says, "under the illusion that people were looking for new ways to be able to approach the corporate power structure, but I found that nobody was looking for a new direction."

Linzey wanted to see his evolving ideas implemented at the grassroots level in the communities that were beginning to ask him for help. In the spring of 1995, with his partner Stacey Schmader and his former law professor Brenda Sue Thornton, he created the Community Environmental Legal Defense Fund (CELDF). CELDF began to help people in various communities research environmental laws and prepare for permit appeals. By

1997, the majority of CELDF's clients were community groups that were fighting against something they didn't want—a factory farm, an incinerator, or maybe a new WalMart. Warned that he would never make a go of a "nonprofit" law firm, Linzey never turned anyone down, and after a few lean years, CELDF became solvent when it was given a fat check by an opponent to a highway project in Virginia.

Construction of the Virginia highway project meant blowing apart a mountain and wreaking havoc in southwestern Virginia's pristine and historic Ellett Valley, which happened to be two miles away from where Linzey's father still lived. At the time, Linzey believed in the effectiveness of the National Environmental Policy Act, a law established to "create and maintain conditions under which man and nature can exist in productive harmony." Over time, CELDF brought forth five lawsuits. They lost in every ruling. Linzey concludes:

> The National Environmental Policy Act requires environmental impact statements for any project that uses federal money. But there is no accompanying legal requirement to select the least environmentally destructive course of action. The act is supposed to inform decision makers, yet it is not binding in any way on the decision. So, really, it's a pointless expenditure of money that gives people the illusion that something is being done to protect the environment.

At the highway's ceremonial ground breaking, Linzey and his friends disrupted the event. Speaking through a bullhorn from the back of a pickup truck, he read out a "Eulogy For Ellett Valley," and was thrown in jail. (This "road to nowhere" still doesn't connect to anything and has caused wide-scale water losses throughout the region.)

In 2001, Linzey and Schmader bought a twenty-four-foot RV that functioned as a mobile law office. Driving all around rural Pennsylvania with their mutt, Dio, in tow, they provided free legal services to people with little resources. Even though they were successful in their appeals at the extraordinary rate of 174 to 1, corporations would always come back and fix the legal holes revealed by the appeal, and would then be granted license to install whatever it was the particular community was fighting against. "So we got awards and funding," Linzey says, "we got accolades and looked wonderful on paper, but in the end, the communities were losing and getting what they didn't want."

Then calls began to come in from local governments in rural Pennsylvania that were trying to stop factory hog farms from inundating their communities and bringing with them economic and environmental harms. The hog farm corporations were taking advantage of a 1993 state law, the Nutrient Management Act, which effectively nullified the local manure-management ordinances of over four hundred communities. Instead of assisting these communities to file the expected permit appeals to this new state law, CELDF decided to instead work with them to pioneer another approach—one focused on asserting the right of local community members to define the type of agriculture they wanted within their community. Linzey explains:

> Regulatory programs are drafted by the corporations that benefit from them. It's the agribusiness corporations that control the regulatory framework of factory farms coming in, so we're faced with a system of laws, and it took us six years to truly understand that this is a system of law—which allows a board of directors to have more rights than five thousand people in the community.

Following the lead of nine Midwestern states, CELDF began to draft local ordinances that prohibited agribusiness corporations from "engaging in farming" within a municipality. This represented the first effort at changing the focus from merely regulating environmental harms to subordinating corporations to local community control. The tiny rural community of Wells Township, Fulton County, became the first municipality to adopt such an ordinance. Five other townships in Fulton County followed over the next year.

Linzey found himself continually spending more and more time on the phone with people who wanted to know if he could help them, and if what CELDF was doing could be replicated in their own municipality. During one of these conversations, the caller suggested that they start a school. In the spring of 2003, Linzey and colleagues taught the first "Daniel Pennock Democracy School," named in honor of Danny Pennock, a teenager from Berks County, Pennsylvania, who died of sludge poisoning.

The Democracy School examines the way the United States Constitution was written, how it was anchored in an English structure of law, and how the Supreme Court has slowly interpreted it to enshrine the rights of corporations into settled law. The school explores a number of those judicial interpretations, which have led to the Bill of Rights protecting corporations from everyday citizens.

Many participants in the Democracy School already know that the Fourteenth Amendment to the United States Constitution, ". . . nor shall any State deprive any person of life, liberty, or property, without due process of law; nor deny to any person within its jurisdiction the equal protection of the laws," was passed to guarantee the rights of recently freed slaves. What many don't know is that, in the late 1800s, this amendment was also applied to protect railroad corporations. In *Santa Clara County v. Southern Pacific Railroad,* the Supreme Court ruled that "we are all of the opinion that the Fourteenth Amendment does apply to the corporation." In essence, the Supreme Court endowed human rights to an *entity of property.* When participants in the Democracy

School learn this fact, they come to understand why the inhabitants of a particular community cannot simply decide, for example, that longwall mining or a big-box store or a factory farm is destructive to the local environment, and therefore must not be allowed in the community.

The Democracy School also explores how equal rights movements have brought about positive change by altering laws and driving new rights into the United States Constitution. There is a lot to be learned from the suffrage and abolitionist movements, as well as from the lesser-known populist and labor movements, that can help us today. In the school's final sessions, people discuss how they can integrate forms of rights-based organizing into a plan or campaign that addresses the issues of their particular locality. These issues are reframed so that, instead of *fighting against* something, participants are asked to describe what they are *fighting for*, and to create a vision of the community they want to bring into existence.

When the school is completed and the participants return home, CELDF then assists them in drafting local laws aimed at achieving their goals for their community, and works with community leaders to adopt those laws. "Today," Linzey says, "it is our communities and natural systems that are treated as property under the law—just as slaves once were—because people living in communities can't control their own futures, and what's in our communities is routinely bought, sold, and traded without a whisker of local control. In many ways, this work is about walking in the footsteps of those prior movements to transform ourselves from being property under the law to becoming people who harness the power of government to defend and enforce our rights."

What follows in these pages is a systematic set of lessons that these communities learned, supported by a collection of individual and community stories that can serve as a guide for both concerned citizens and experienced activists looking for a new strategy. This form of organizing is unique in defying the usual red state–blue state or liberal versus conservative delineations, and brings people together in defense of their common needs. Each community portrayed here is not begging its government to give it more rights, but rather is manifesting new rights for itself through lawmaking at the local level. Legally, they are being, to paraphrase the famous Gandhi quote, the change they want to see.

In so doing, these people have learned from prior citizens' movements that have openly challenged and then changed unjust laws, such as those denying "personhood" rights to vast numbers of people. Today's dire threats to the environment, and thus human survival, require equally daring measures.

As you look through this book, you may not find the exact threat you face, or a law spelled out that fits your community's particular situation. The principles expressed, however, are the same for all communities. It all starts with a conversation. The first question to ask and answer is: Who decides what happens in my community? Once you discover the answer to this question, the path becomes clear.

While changing long-settled governmental structures may seem daunting, we can be inspired by one small country that has blazed the way. The government of Ecuador, working along with Thomas Linzey and CELDF, has recently established a new constitution—the first in the world that grants nature the inalienable right "to exist, persist, maintain and regenerate its vital cycles, structure, functions, and its processes in evolution."

Now it's your turn.

— Anneke Campbell

You will note that Thomas Linzey is referred to in the third person throughout this book. I worked closely with him to accurately represent his work and the work of the Community Environmental Legal Defense Fund.

Chapter 1

THE ILLUSION
OF DEMOCRACY

Lessons Learned

- *The established system of government does not protect your community. Be willing to try a new approach in order to reclaim your voice.*

- *Change begins at the grassroots level. Talk with neighbors and community members, encouraging communication and debate.*

- *Attend town meetings to know what changes are being planned for your community, and to prevent unwanted decisions from being made.*

T he history of our progress as a people has always involved unhappy citizens coming together to improve their lives. Over the years this organizing has taken many forms in pressuring our government to expand citizens' rights and protections; not all modes of organizing work for all conditions and times. Therefore, when working to create change, organizers need to continually evaluate whether their current approach is effective. An approach that has worked well in the past might now be outdated or ineffective, but this is not necessarily easy to recognize or admit. So it is with our system of environmental law and protection, which is shrouded in a belief in both its effectiveness and its excellence. In order to create true change, citizens must learn to recognize the complex structure of laws and governance that buffers corporations, which often control the decisions affecting an overall community.

It's never easy to question the prevailing beliefs of our times. Most of us accept without question the idea that we live in a democracy.

Webster's dictionary defines a democracy as a form of government in which the supreme power is vested in the people and exercised directly by them or by their elected agents; it also states that in a democratic state, decisions are made by the common people, as distinguished from any privileged class. What the people in Blaine Township, Pennsylvania, came to realize was that one such "privileged class"—in this case, a mining company's board of directors—had more power to decide what happened in the community than did its own residents.

Blaine Township versus the Coal Companies

Blaine Township is a small rural township about forty-five miles west of Pittsburgh, in Washington County. The racial makeup of the township is overwhelmingly white, and the majority of people live in Taylorstown, a one-stop-sign town. There are a total of twenty-two square miles within the municipality. Although Blaine is dotted with farms, a lot of the farms were razed after a proposed power plant moved in and bought them up. Many people moved away.

Blaine is crossed by Buffalo Creek, a high-quality perennial stream that flows into West Virginia and dumps into the Ohio River. Its banks are scented by wildflowers and pervaded by the sounds of crickets and cicadas, and spanning the creek is the historic Saw Hill covered bridge, made of red wooden slats. A mile and a half down the road is a Revolutionary War fort called Williamson's Station. The township is a haven to sportsmen of all stripes—fishermen, birders, people who come to train their dogs for hunting—and the fees paid by hunters are a major source of income for the community.

Western Pennsylvania has been mining coal for 250 years, but no mining has ever occurred in Blaine, and its residents and township supervisors aim to keep it that way.

Longwall Mining Approaches Blaine

The Pittsburgh coal seam, of which the Buffalo Reserve is a part, lies directly beneath Blaine. Coal companies purchased the rights to this coal a hundred years ago, putting the decision to early residents like this: "We're going to give you money for something we're probably not going to come for in your lifetime." In a poor county, few passed up an offer like that.

Recently, Blaine Township resident and planning board member Michael Vacca became aware that the Consol Energy Company wanted to mine in Blaine. Neighboring communities were experiencing one of the newest trends in coal removal: longwall coal mining. The procedure for longwall coal mining goes something like this: six to eight hundred feet below the earth's surface, depending on the seam, a machine moves across the face of the coal, grinding it up at tremendous speed. After the machines come through and remove the coal, the earth drops three to six feet above the seam. This is called *subsidence*. The damage created by subsidence has caused the practice of longwall mining to be banned in Germany—the country where it originated.

Muscular, with long sandy hair and a goatee, Michael Vacca looks like he might have stepped out of a book about the Wild West. He pours cement for a living and does not call himself an activist or an environmentalist, even though much of his time has been spent organizing both his own as well as surrounding communities in order to protect and conserve nature. He's a can-do kind of guy, knowledgeable and practical. When he bought his house thirty years ago, he planted trees to shelter the place from sun, wind, and snow. He also built six windmills so that he could be independent from the grid.

Vacca saw that longwall mining was leaving communities decimated in its wake—aquifers dewatered, streams and rivers destroyed, historic buildings sunk into the ground, and local wells replaced with gray plastic tanks of water called water buffaloes, which squat like big gray lumps in a yard. Some people in Blaine had relatives or friends whose communities had been mined and the lands devastated, and who were then left to deal with the consequences.

Vacca cares deeply about the place that supports his life. He knows the Buffalo Creek watershed is the last contiguous forested floodplain in Washington County, as well as a critical habitat for neotropical migrating birds. The pristine watershed is home to many creatures that only breed in high-quality water—certain salamanders, for instance. There is no public water in the county, so everyone draws water from the ground. The Clean Stream Act states that nobody may destroy a water source or not restore a stream to its original state. But a lot of times the only means of "restoration" involves pouring concrete, which means that mosses and ponds—the basis of stream life and habitat—are lost. Other times, "restoration" means running a pipe from one stream into another, which does nothing for a stream whose headwaters have already been destroyed. Clearly, the law doesn't work to protect the streams in actuality.

Michael Vacca is proudly computer illiterate. He spent months researching the harmful effects of longwall mining, learning that, during the 1990s, the state of Pennsylvania changed the state laws so that subsidence was built into mining permits, making it legal. In this area, as they say, coal is king.

> MICHAEL VACCA: Coalfield environmental-activist groups advised us to appeal the permits issued by the Department of Environmental Protection to at least get a better deal on oil, gas, and coal leases. It seemed we had no choice in the matter, and that the only thing we could do was try to make the incursion of longwall mining as non-invasive as possible. I knew from my own past experience that this too was going to fail.

Previous Environmental Threats to Community

Vacca had already battled environmental threats to his community. In 1999, Allegheny Power wanted to build a power plant in the beautiful valley just down the road from Saw Hill Bridge. Residents found out about the plan when the county lifted the covered bridge off its moorings and placed steel beams underneath it, so that it would be ready to carry truck traffic and construction workers. Later, they discovered that both their county and state agencies had known about the project for years (state legislators had continually courted mining lobbyists) but did not give them any notice. The energy generated by the plant would not service local communities, but instead would be sold to whoever would pay the highest price.

Vacca formed a group to fight the power plant through the regulatory system—in this instance, the Department of Environmental Protection. Since this agency issues permits, it soon became clear that there was little protection and much "permitting." Nevertheless, Vacca and friends raised funds and engaged an attorney and biologists to study the area. They applied for designation as an Important Bird Area with the Audubon Society. An archeologist was asked to research whether Williamson Station could be placed on a list of historic sites.

The group went through several rounds at different courts, petitioning and re-petitioning, losing again and again. After all their efforts, they were not even allowed to introduce environmental impact studies in their case. Then they got lucky. The energy market suddenly stopped its expansion, and Allegheny Power decided to sell the land to the game commission. In order to prevent similar threats from arising in the future, Vacca decided to become a member of the town planning commission. To his chagrin, he discovered that Pennsylvania state municipal code *required* communities to make an allowance for any kind of commercial development.

> MICHAEL VACCA: I discovered that we cannot say no. Since most of the subsurface mineral rights had already been bought, they were done deals from a lease standpoint. The best the other townships could do was to

raise the fees or to try to get a higher price. But to me, this place is priceless.

Another local resident with a home she considers priceless is Karen Duerr, an attractive young woman with long dark hair and brown eyes that exude calm. Duerr has lived all of her twenty-seven years in an old brick farmhouse with a lovely front porch and a number of outbuildings, including an ancient silo. Hens chase their baby chicks around the yard. Her property stretches for a hundred acres, and is bordered on one edge by Buffalo Creek. Karen and her family grow and harvest hay, part of which they keep for their own animals, selling the rest to local farmers.

Like many other brick houses in the area, Karen's home has a very old foundation, which doesn't take well to subsidence. She knows that if longwall mining takes place, the foundation of her home will most likely crumble. She also knows that longwall mining will compromise the area's water supply and destroy her beloved Buffalo Creek. As a little girl, Karen was always down at the creek; when it got dark outside, her parents knew where to find her.

KAREN DUERR: I love this place. I've lived here my whole life. My parents live here. This is my home and I don't want to see it destroyed.

Karen's father grew up in heavily polluted Pittsburgh, but he always dreamed of being a farmer. After he bought land in Blaine

Township, he became a township supervisor, working to make conservation a reality. This brought him into battle with the Pennzoil Company, which owns the rights to the oil under many farms in Blaine. The company reopened two old oil wells on the Duerr family property, its right-of-way putting a driveway right through the pasture. Although Karen's father and others spent much of the mid-1980s raising money and meeting time and time again to fight against oil drilling, they could never prove substantively that Pennzoil was responsible for the erosion of their topsoil or the contamination of their water by petroleum leaks. The burden of proof required constant and expensive testing by scientists. And while contamination by Pennzoil was finally demonstrated, the company had on staff full-time lawyers whose job consisted of throwing doubt on the findings and claiming that it was the company, and not the community, which was facing discrimination.

> KAREN DUERR: At the time, of course, I didn't know what the basis was that these corporations keep winning on. I was tired of complaining about it and wanted to do something, but I didn't know what. Then Michael Vacca came over and invited us to attend a Democracy School. I was cynical at that point, but I trusted Michael.

Group Turns to CELDF to Help Fight Assault

In his work on the planning board, Michael Vacca had started to update and upgrade the Blaine Township zoning ordinance. He figured that if he couldn't stop mining, he could at least try to minimize the damage. He was looking for the most restrictive language that would pass legal muster when someone referred him to the Community Environmental Legal Defense Fund. Vacca had a long talk with Thomas Linzey.

After Vacca explained the apparent rigging of the regulatory system against local communities, Linzey asked him a question: "If the regulatory and land-use laws can't stop the mining, are you willing to try something different?"

Linzey offered to hold a Democracy School in Blaine, explaining that the community needed to get educated about the current realities of democracy and self-governance. Vacca made a list of people he thought should attend, including farmers and local government officials. One of the people he connected with was Fred Cramer.

> FRED CRAMER: My home is 156 years old. It will be destroyed if it is mined. I will lose everything I came to Blaine Township for: my quality of life, my retirement, my life savings, everything. And Blaine Township will lose its emergency water supply, which is my pond. I wanted to find out: Why don't we have a say in what happens here?

Group Identifies Root Cause of Problem

The three-day Democracy School was an eye opener for all who attended. They learned about how the United States Constitution was written behind closed doors by thirty-nine white men of property, who represented their interests in the document at the expense of the rights and interests of 90 percent of the people. In fact, rather than trusting people to self-govern, many of our founding fathers didn't trust the people, believing, as James Madison did, that monarchy was the best form of government.

On the second day of the school, participants delved into how judicial interpretations have led to the establishing of corporate "personhood," which has ultimately resulted in the Bill of Rights protecting corporations from the will of the people.

> KAREN DUERR: When I attended Democracy School, I learned a lot that I didn't learn during my years of education. I didn't know that corporations are considered persons in the eyes of the law.

While corporations possess the same rights under the United States Constitution as ordinary citizens, they are not legally bound to respect people's constitutional rights. This is so because constitutional rights were written to shield people from invasive governmental action (e.g., the First Amendment, "Congress shall pass no law . . ."), not corporate action. But because corporate decision makers are not governmental officials, *corporations cannot be sued for violating a person's constitutional rights.*

Blaine Township's three supervisors—Scott Weiss, Darlene Dutton and Jim McElheny—also attended the school. Scott Weiss, the chairman of the supervisors, is the manager of a testing company. He has lived in Blaine Township for thirty years. He is a bright and energetic father of two daughters. Darlene Dutton is a recovery-room nurse, and a mom and a grandmother. Jim McElheny, now retired, has been a truck driver and a minister. He now takes care of his grandkids.

> SCOTT WEISS: It is shocking that corporations are seen as people. They're using our own amendments against us.

> DARLENE DUTTON: This country has devalued me as a human being in relation to corporations. They have given these companies the same rights that people have, and these rights end up trumping ours. We need to say enough is enough. We start small and we start changing this country.

Participants in the Democracy School also learned about the United States Constitution's "commerce clause," and how it is applied today.

Communities are not allowed to inhibit commerce, and just about anything can be defined as commerce.

The commerce clause enables corporations to sue local and state governments when those governments adopt laws seeking to control or regulate commerce. This structure of law prevents people from implementing their visions of environmentally and economically sustainable communities.

Group Decides on New Rights-Based Course of Organizing

Something communities under this kind of threat or assault have in common is that they come together in reaction to a specific issue. They spend all their energies pushing against what they *don't want,* rather than asking themselves what they *do want.* In Democracy School, the conversation shifts so that people begin to ask: What kind of community do we want to live in? And what are we going to do to bring our vision for our community into being? The Blaine residents returned over and over to their main concern: Who decides what happens in Blaine?

The Blaine Township supervisors are responsible not only for the fiscal operations of the township, the township roads, and maintaining order, but also for following and maintaining a community vision. Considering the area's state game lands, these supervisors want their community to promote outdoor activities. They have a freshwater creek, some old-forest growth, an aviary, and a lot of wildlife. This is exactly the type of community they want to maintain. When they each became a supervisor, they took an oath to look after the welfare of the township and its people.

When the coal company started encroaching in the surrounding communities, the Blaine supervisors knew it was just a matter of time until their community was encroached on as well. At one time, Darlene Dutton used to think that mining could be regulated and controlled. Then she started seeing evidence all around her to the contrary. She soon realized you "get what you try to regulate."

The supervisors in Blaine noticed the majority of people in other communities didn't get motivated until they had already lost what they held dear. As elected representatives, they realized they had to have the foresight to protect their community.

They decided to be proactive to prevent the loss of property, water, and habitat. And to do that, they knew they had to think innovatively.

> MICHAEL VACCA: We had sample ordinances from CELDF. We examined the language contained in them. We were asking real, specific questions. What we liked about these ordinances was that they gave the power to the people. They are rights-based. Those of us who live and pay taxes here would be exercising our right to decide.

Group Codifies New Vision into Laws or Legal Structures

The township supervisors brainstormed and asked Thomas Linzey to write an ordinance banning longwall mining. The language came from all who were present during the discussions. Basically, the ordinance states that to protect the health, safety, and general welfare of the township, no corporation has the right to come and mine within township boundaries, or to harm the ecosystem within it.

Representatives Support New Structures

Once the supervisors unanimously approved the ordinance, it needed to be advertised, and then a time set for public comment. Michael Vacca, Karen Duerr, and other active Blaine residents

The Ordinance's Introduction

An ordinance to protect the health, safety, and general welfare of the citizens and natural environment of Blaine Township by banning corporations from engaging in mining within the township; by banning corporate ownership of land and mineral estates used for mining within the township; by banning persons from using corporations to engage in mining; by banning the exercise of certain powers by mining corporations; by recognizing the rights of ecosystems and natural communities and by providing for enforcement of those rights.

went to all the meetings and spread the word further in the township. A lot of people got involved after being personally contacted and invited to the meetings. Blaine residents asked whether something similar had been done in other communities, and CELDF provided information about townships that had passed similar kinds of ordinances with success. Some Pennsylvania communities, for instance, had banned corporate sludge dumping, and not one ounce of sludge had been spread on the land.

At the meeting for public comment, most people judged the new ordinance a good thing. Many were thankful that the supervisors were standing up for the environment. They were also concerned about infrastructure problems, as they had paid good money for their wells and septic systems. Only two people spoke against the ordinance—a representative from the coal company and an attorney, who threatened the supervisors with lawsuits. The supervisors had to prepare themselves, not only for a possible suit against the township, but also that they could be sued personally. The support CELDF offered was reassuring.

DARLENE DUTTON: We'll deal with whatever they bring on. The support of my friends and family gives me strength, but my faith is first.

SCOTT WEISS: It also helps that we are united and have a lot of respect for each other. We're not going to let them divide the three of us.

Community Passes Ordinance into Local Law

The supervisors unanimously passed the ordinance. Then, realizing that it could not stand alone if it came to a challenge, they passed a second ordinance stripping corporations of the right to be considered persons. In essence, they removed legal powers and privileges from corporations at the municipal level, creating a protective barrier for the community against the threat of coal mining.

Coal Company Propaganda

In return, the coal-mining company made a variety of efforts to curry favor in the region, including building a ballpark and bombarding the community with advertisements offering the promise of "clean" coal.

> DARLENE DUTTON: My grandchildren brought home coloring books donated to the school from the coal company. There were pages with Frosty the Snowman with coal eyes, a father and mother thanking [the coal company] for electricity. It introduced the kids to all the terms used in mining and how it powers their video games. But they don't show how there's no more water!

Scott Weiss deplored the propaganda because it made the real conversation democracy requires even more difficult. The community supervisors were accused by the coal company of standing in the path of progress and energy. But the supervisors were clear on this point: A corporation's ability to make a profit from a coal mine does not give it the right to ruin a community.

MICHAEL VACCA: In the end, you have to call it like it is. Are we going to prostitute ourselves? For what are we willing to sell ourselves, our land, our water?

Group Expands Education and Deepens Commitment
Once the ordinance passed, the next phase of the work began. Michael Vacca and local residents Jim Powell and Fred Cramer formed the Buffalo Creek Conservation Association. Their hope was that communities facing the same threat would be willing to empower themselves by passing ordinances of their own, which would in turn strengthen the entire region. They sent letters to the other townships in Washington County, explaining how longwall mining works, telling them that it was coming to their area, and describing the Blaine ordinance. Vacca attended twenty-two township meetings to discuss the ordinance and invited citizens to come talk to the people in Blaine. There were few takers.

JIM POWELL: People have that classic response: you can't win, this is the way it's been, this is the way it's going to be, don't ask me to help. That is a very significant ball and chain to dislodge, to get people to stick their head out of the box, when they're used to getting whacked and have become accepting of their fate.

Besides resignation, the media often presents another obstacle in the attempt to create change.

Mainstream media, which usually operates under the assumption that "progress" is necessary and good, often does not inform the public of their rights or allow for healthy debate.

It instead puts up a screen of propaganda, forcing people to take time to educate themselves—if they take any time at all. Yet another obstacle to change is the threat of losing jobs.

> MICHAEL VACCA: It's hard to get past the jobs thing. No miner wants to lose his or her job. In some communities, the mine has been the main source of jobs for a long time, so it's built into the culture.

Coal companies use the threat of job loss to pit labor against environmental protection. But the reality is that the number of jobs in the coal industry has fallen by half due to mechanization. And longwall mining will take away other, more sustainable jobs, like farming. But in the end, this is not about stopping mining, it's about who gets to decide.

It's hard to say whether other townships will take up the fight. In order for organizing to be successful, a critical mass has to occur, which means that a majority of people in a community has to stand behind the effort to pass new laws. Often these new laws will go against previously established laws, challenging local and state governments in ways they have never before been challenged. At some point during the fight, it will become clear that, contrary to all they have been taught, everyday citizens do not have the right to govern themselves. That in itself will be a hugely educational moment—one to vaporize illusions in the struggle for a real, live democracy.

> KAREN DUERR: It's about our voice. Democracy means having a voice in the decisions that affect you. We know there's going to be a fight, that we're going to go to court. And if we stand up and win some of these cases, then we'll have a precedent.

> MICHAEL VACCA: There's victory in the challenge. I can tell you that the regulatory fight is one that citizens will never win. With local governance, you pick the fight, you pick the best ground, the high ground. If you choose to govern yourselves, you're making your stand on your own terms as opposed to going begging. This is the stuff the American Revolution left unfinished. We owe it to those people to finish the job.

Chapter 2

RECLAIMING THE DECLARATION OF INDEPENDENCE

Lessons Learned

- *Research your community's founding documents in order to understand your basic rights.*

- *Encourage and inspire local representatives to follow the will of the people, not politicians or corporations.*

- *Work to pass new laws or legal structures that reinforce your vision. Organize a core group and work to prevent unwanted decisions from being made rather than reacting to them after the fact.*

S ometimes referred to as "blue gold," water has become an increasingly precious resource on our warming, crowded planet. In many states, water is a subject of heated struggle between those outside the community who want to sell it for profit and residents who want to protect it. The unfortunate truth learned by many communities is that they have little or no control over their own water resources. In order to gain control, they have to be willing to try a new approach.

While some activism in the United States happens independent of historical understanding, many activists look for lessons from the past in order to not repeat mistakes and to take advantage of what has already been learned. One way they can do this is by examining the documents that govern their community, such as a state constitution, and then learning how to use those documents to strengthen local control and protect the environment.

While many state constitutions have been amended to give corporations more rights than individual communities, they also often contain some stellar resources that support the effort to take back our inalienable rights.

The Towns of Nottingham and Barnstead, New Hampshire

Situated in the middle of the state of New Hampshire, Nottingham and Barnstead are rural communities dating back to the early 1700s. They are about eighteen miles apart, with just under four thousand residents each. Among Nottingham's grantees was Peregrine White, descendant of the first child of English parentage born in New England. According to the United States Census Bureau, water comprises 4 percent of the town's 48.4 square miles. Containing fourteen lakes and ponds, Nottingham is drained by the Pawtuckaway and North rivers, and at one time had seventeen water mills in operation. Not far away, the town of

Barnstead in Belknap County is nearly as water rich, lying within the Merrimack River watershed. In summer you can see kids jumping off the town bridge into the river or swinging by a rope from a tree branch far into the middle of the water. With its large grassy commons bordered by white Victorian homes and lush woods, Barnstead recalls an earlier, more idyllic time.

Given the abundance of good water, it's no wonder this part of New Hampshire has been targeted by a handful of water corporations that want to suck a commodity out of the ground that sells at a price higher than that of raw crude oil.

However, these small towns are also places where democracy is still practiced at the local level, in the form of town meetings. In the state of New Hampshire, the annual town meeting is a forum for community decision-making in which elected representatives, called selectmen, answer directly to those they represent. Any registered resident may attend a town meeting and vote on every article brought up for discussion. Here decisions, budgetary and otherwise, are made; here officials are elected or selected; here ordinances are passed. Some town meetings can get rowdy, and some even stretch into the following day.

Environmental Assault Threatens Community

A company known as USA Springs wanted to put in three wells to withdraw over 430,000 gallons of water a day from the local aquifer for a massive water-bottling operation. These wells were to be situated at the headwaters of Nottingham and nearby Barrington, where most inhabitants rely on wells for their own water supply. USA Springs approached the Nottingham planning board to get the necessary permits. On the first pass, the board, believing that the plant would bring business to Nottingham and add to the tax base, changed the zoning of the property from residential to commercial. As time went on, many Nottingham residents objected, insisting that the plan presented a threat to water quality as well as quantity, and the hearings got volatile. Citizens brought in experts who showed that the operation would drain the bedrock aquifer, pollute the remaining water, and disturb wetlands and wildlife.

Community Group Battles Regulatory System

In response to the actions of USA Springs, an umbrella citizens' group called Save Our Groundwater (SOG) formed in Nottingham and Barrington. Active in SOG was a young woman named Olivia Zink, who was studying for a degree in political science at the University of New Hampshire. She jumped in with both feet to help battle USA Springs.

> OLIVIA ZINK: Who owns our water? This company intended to take 430,000 gallons a day to ship overseas to Italy for profit. This really fascinated me, and I wanted to learn more.

So Zink learned how to be an organizer, how to share information, and how to work with media, businesspeople, neighbors, and elected officials. "It's all about developing those relationships," she says. SOG hired lawyers and familiarized itself with the state's permitting system. The group met with the governor and state representatives, and learned that there were seven other water-bottling plants going in around the state. In response, SOG helped submit legislation to declare that water is held in the public trust, which was passed by the New Hampshire House of Representatives.

In the meantime, USA Springs went to the New Hampshire Department of Environmental Services, which turned down their permit on twenty-seven counts. A water-draw test showed how in just ten days, even while pumping less water than the proposed operation, the wells in the neighborhood dropped forty feet. USA Springs lawyers said there was nothing to worry about, and that they would fix whatever problems arose. But the startling water-draw test results unified people in the affected communities, and it helped SOG cross political and social boundaries and become strong enough to raise funds to mount a legal case. The test also revealed that the pumping had drawn contaminants deeper into the aquifer. Under the New Hampshire Groundwater Protection Act, these contaminants were considered to have an adverse impact. The Department of Environmental Services denied the permit a second time.

SOG celebrated. USA Springs appealed. One of the reasons for the denial from the Department of Environmental Services was that property adjacent to the site contained buried toxins from a large truck-repair facility. USA Springs bought the additional property and filled in the well with chemicals to decontaminate the area. On the company's third application, the permit was approved. The other twenty-six reasons for the earlier denial were disregarded.

Once the necessary parts of the new permit application were filled in, the community planning board had no real ability to fight back, and the company was given the permit to start pumping. Zink was appalled to realize that USA Springs had received permission to literally steal the community's water.

Local Government Says: "Nothing We Can Do"

After the Department of Environmental Services reversed its decision and issued the new permit, the Nottingham elected officials, called the select board, told the community there was nothing further they could do. A second group, Neighborhood Guardians, formed to fight the development of USA Springs. Together with

SOG, they continued to battle USA Springs through the regulatory system, losing the case on every single permit.

At one point, when USA Springs applied for a new driveway permit, the police chief went to the hearing and spoke on the dangers of having trucks pull out every three minutes and the disastrous effect of fully loaded trucks driving the main thoroughfare between Concord and Plymouth. He was told he had no standing. Neither did any other community group. Only USA Springs had standing to testify, and they said it was their right to draw water from their land. After years of appeals, the case ended up squarely in front of the New Hampshire Supreme Court.

Group Turns to CELDF to Help Fight Threat

Zink could see that her activism wasn't accomplishing the results she was looking for. She brought Thomas Linzey to New Hampshire to present the Democracy School to local communities.

> OLIVIA ZINK: I saw that we had to start focusing on who was making the decisions. The fight was about water, but it was really deeper than that. It was about who decides what our community looks like.

Barnstead Takes Note

In the meantime, the people in Barnstead had been witnessing what was happening in Nottingham, where so many tax dollars were being spent fighting USA Springs, and in Alton, another community nearby, where a smaller bottling plant was already operational. Barnstead's concerned citizens invited SOG to come have a discussion. Zink showed *Thirst*, a documentary about how companies took water from locally built ponds in India and then sold the water back to the very people who had dug the ponds in the first place. Zink compared this example to what was happening in Nottingham, where the regulatory system had failed to help citizens. She asked the people of Barnstead, "Do you really want to spend energy and community resources battling something you won't win, or do you want to try a different way?" To strengthen her case, she talked about how multiple communities in Pennsylvania, along with help from CELDF, had recently passed ordinances successfully banning corporations from spreading sludge waste.

This drew the attention of Barnstead resident Gail Darrell because Barnstead had previously passed a resolution against corporate sludge-spreading, but it did not stop the practice. She also knew that people in various other communities were passing resolutions to protect their water but were having no success. Darrell sought more information. A New Hampshire native, homesteader, and gardener, she was a stay-at-home mom, raising her four children and her vegetables in the quiet countryside. She lives in a rustic old home with a welcoming kitchen, where a pot of soup is always simmering on the woodstove. The river runs 150 yards from the house and the well sits right by the kitchen door, supplying both house and garden. She worried that if the water-bottling plant drained the local aquifer, the area's farmers and their animals would be severely affected.

After attending Democracy School, Darrell learned that the regulatory system is set up to create a barrier between local citizens and corporate entities. This barrier isn't some kind of malfunction; it's built into the system.

> GAIL DARRELL: If you have corporations that come into your town, and you do not have a say, you do not live in a democracy. We should start acting like sovereign people who can have an impact and a perspective!

Zink noticed the avid interest from the Barnstead residents.

> OLIVIA ZINK: Democracy School is a good tool, but it's using that tool to inform your community that matters. The first school in Barnstead spurred on conversations at the community store, and the town hall, and while pumping gas. That first night, people didn't sleep, they pulled out the constitution, and returned in the morning, excited and motivated to keep learning.

Group Decides on Rights-Based Course of Organizing

Darrell and other citizens formed a core-group committee with the goal of bringing to the select board a real plan for protecting Barnstead's water. A core-group committee is composed of about ten people at any given time.

To organize effectively, you need a core of people who understand the issue, but it is usually the three or four people who have a little more discretionary time who keep the ball rolling.

Darrell was one such person. She had lived in the town for many years, and she had a good reputation, so she went door to door, talking to every neighbor, and then she traveled further into outlying areas. She talked people into attending public meetings. She told them about the situation in Nottingham and how Barnstead was trying a new approach.

> GAIL DARRELL: The most important part of organizing is the day-to-day conversations with neighbors around kitchen tables. That's what builds a strong movement, sharing information and expertise and opinions. The great thing is that people begin to talk, not only about what they are against, but more importantly, what they want their community to look like and what rights they believe they possess.

The Barnstead select board met with Thomas Linzey, who asked what the group wanted to do. Selectman Gordon Preston said, "We want you to write us an ordinance," and Selectman Jack

O'Neill said, "And we want it to start it with 'We the People.' "

Unified, the governing body of Barnstead agreed they wanted to start their ordinance with a preamble citing that their authority comes from the Declaration of Independence, which declares that governments are instituted to secure people's rights, and that government derives its just powers from the consent of the governed.

PREAMBLE of Barnstead's Ordinance of Rights

Section 2. Preamble and Purpose.

We the People of the Town of Barnstead declare that water is essential for life, liberty, and the pursuit of happiness—both for people and for the ecological systems, which give life to all species. We the People of the Town of Barnstead declare that we have the duty to safeguard the water both on and beneath the Earth's surface, and in the process, safeguard the rights of people within the community of Barnstead, and the rights of the ecosystems of which Barnstead is a part. We the people of Barnstead declare that all of our water is held in the public trust as a common resource to be used for the benefit of Barnstead residents and of the natural ecosystems of which they are a part.

Community Gathers Support for the Ordinance

Among the many people who worked hard to get the ordinance passed were Bruce Shearer and Carolyn Namaste, a couple who have chosen to raise some of their own food and to live close to the land. They strongly believe that they have to practice what they preach when it comes to protecting nature.

> BRUCE SHEARER: We're part of the whole living web of life. But the government represents money. I'm not saying there are no good politicians, but really, who's calling the shots?

It comes down to who decides here, we the people or we the money.

Selectman Jack O'Neill became one of the ordinance's strongest advocates. Initially, he had supported USA Springs because Barnstead needed the business. But the more he learned about the company's plan, the less he could support it. He decided to personally educate the community, writing letters to the editor, joining in potluck dinners and meetings at the library, publishing articles to keep people informed, and speaking at the American Legion. He helped sway the other four selectmen of the planning board with the argument that if they had an ordinance in place, USA Springs would not spend a half-million dollars on legal fees, but would instead be motivated to go elsewhere. Thomas Linzey and CELDF had already committed to stand by Barnstead and fight any legal battles that ensued.

An Obstacle: People's Unwillingness to Break Illegal Law

Gail Darrell and other members of her group spent a year of solid organizing, informing community members about the issue and attending every town meeting to remind the select board of their duty to do the will of the people. One obstacle she had not planned on encountering was the concern on the part of many citizens, as well as the selectmen, to move against the laws that grant corporations personhood rights. Her group realized that, for some people, going up against established law was a huge and often frightening challenge. Some people got angry with Darrell, reacting negatively to her message. She told them that throughout American history, people have had to challenge settled laws that violate community and human rights. She also assured them that the ordinance did not violate their state constitution.

The Vote in Barnstead

Darrell and Shearer both agree that if neighboring Nottingham hadn't already set the example of how much taxpayer money could be wasted using the regulatory system, the Barnstead ordinance probably would not have passed.

When there is a situation close to home that people can identify with, they are more attentive.

At Barnstead's annual town meeting, the community deemed that the ordinance was the right approach to protect its water, with 135 people voting a resounding "yes" and only one vote against.

Selectman Jack O'Neill, a Vietnam veteran, was proud to pass the ordinance, as was Gordon Preston, who originally moved his family to Barnstead to be near ski country. While wildly different in temperament, both men recognize they have established something that does not simply protect the water in their town, but is groundbreaking law.

> GORDON PRESTON: New Hampshire is a good state to pioneer this law in. Because of our structure of town meetings and the wording of our constitution, our judges are extremely reluctant to go after an existing town vote, so it's therefore unlikely it would be overturned.

> JACK O'NEILL: I went to war for my country. I have to say, this is the first time in my life I've seen democracy starting to work. We the people of Barnstead threw aside our fears for the generations to come, knowing we were in a battle with the corporations and their legal teams. To the nation, this might be a small battle, but something has to be done, and we the people of the town of Barnstead will walk point.

Regulatory System Fails Nottingham

All the while that the people in Barnstead were being proactive in organizing and passing their ordinance, activist groups in Nottingham had high hopes as their case moved forward to be heard in the New Hampshire Supreme Court. They pinned these hopes on the argument that because groundwater is held in the "public trust," the court should prevent abuse of the groundwater system. They argued that the Department of Environmental Services permit violated the public trust because it allowed privatization of the water supplies.

On July 8, 2007, the New Hampshire Supreme Court issued its decision. It denied that the two community groups had standing in the case and unanimously ruled in favor of the corporation and the state, which had filed a brief supporting the corporation.

Some Nottingham residents had anticipated this possible dead-end and started investigating Barnstead's ordinance. Chris and Gail Mills, a long-married couple, attended Democracy School soon after Barnstead passed its ordinance. "I've never gotten involved in doing anything like this before," Chris said, "but I was appalled that USA Springs kept getting permits. I was hoping somebody else would step up, but no one else did, so I said, 'I'll do it myself.' "

The Mills and others decided to form a group (named the Nottingham Tea Party) in order to educate the town and pass an ordinance similar to the one that had passed in Barnstead. The group was composed of Democrats, Republicans, and Independents. They invited speakers into the community, developed publications, and put together brochures. When they started their work, most of the members of the community considered it too late to do anything about USA Springs. So the Nottingham Tea Party created a brochure entitled: IT'S NOT TOO LATE. They made the point that an ordinance would protect them in the future if another corporation should come in. And they created displays with a powerful quote from Abraham Lincoln:

> I see in the near future a crisis approaching that unnerves me and causes me to tremble for the safety of my country. Corporations have been enthroned and an era of corruption in high places will follow, and the money power of the country will endeavor to prolong its reign by working upon the prejudices of the people until all wealth is aggregated in a few hands and the Republic is destroyed.

John Terninko, who has lived in Nottingham for forty-one years and calls himself a "city kid turned country," came onboard when he signed one of the Mills' petitions. His comments at the Department of Environmental Services hearing reflected his frustration: "I recognize that everything I will say is irrelevant. This company [USA Springs] has violated our trust. They have violated seventeen ordinances in Barrington already, which should be sufficient grounds to not do business with them, but that doesn't stop you at DES from moving forward with the permits. This whole process is a sham."

When the Tea Party held group meetings, they invited the members of their select board to attend, but these representatives, unlike those in Barnstead, declined to participate.

Education and Obstacles

In order to get public support for their ordinance, the Tea Party needed to present their information before a town meeting. Since the select board did not provide any backing, the Tea Party was left to its own resources. The group quickly gathered 162 signatures, which they then they presented to the town clerk, who had no choice but to place the issue on the select board's agenda.

In educating Nottingham citizens about the ordinance, the Tea Party organizers faced several obstacles. The first was the assumption that all business is good business because it brings taxes and jobs. The Tea Party had to explain that new jobs are often filled from outside town, and that the town's treasury would be severely taxed to pay for the new costs of infrastructure and pollution. A second obstacle was based on an unwillingness to admit that the government wasn't looking out for the best interests of its citizens. Many people found it hard to give up that hope.

Gail Mills addressed another sticking point:

> Stripping corporations of the rights of persons really confused people. Businesses were getting frightened, calling to say they wouldn't be able to do business in

Nottingham any more. We had to explain that it is when corporations use those rights to get their way that they are doing harm, not when they are doing good business.

The fire department chief expressed his concern that the language of the ordinance meant he wouldn't be able to help out other towns with water. The Tea Party then created an amendment to the ordinance, identifying the exceptions when organizations such as the fire department, local utilities, the military, and nonprofits would be allowed to use and transport water, as long as they didn't sell the water outside Nottingham.

The ordinance presented by the Nottingham Tea Party stated that they were relying on Article 10 of New Hampshire's constitution, written in 1784, which says that government is instituted for the whole community and those who are unhappy have the right to take action.

This is called the "right of revolution."

In other words, government is not constituted for any particular class of men, and when other means of redress are ineffectual, people ought to establish a new government.

The Nottingham Vote

The town meeting lasted from 8 a.m. to 5 p.m., with 365 people in attendance. The select board had the same amount of time to

The right of revolution: Part I, Article 10:

... Government being instituted for the common benefit, protection, and security of the whole community, and not for the private interest or emolument of any one man, family, or class of men; therefore, whenever the ends of government are perverted, and public liberty manifestly endangered, and all other means of redress are ineffectual, the people may, and of right ought to reform the old, or establish a new government. The doctrine of nonresistance against arbitrary power, and oppression, is absurd, slavish, and destructive of the good and happiness of mankind. ...

present its position as the Nottingham Tea Party, during which they tried to discredit Thomas Linzey and the ordinance. Their stance was that the town had spent a lot of money defending lawsuits and didn't want any more money spent on fighting USA Springs, especially now that the company had obtained all its permits. Regardless of the opinion of the select board, the community passed the ordinance with 63 percent of the vote. And to protect it against unilateral action by the select board, a clause was written into the ordinance that two-thirds of the community would be needed to overturn it, and this could not happen without a town meeting. Afterward, the Nottingham Tea Party sent a registered letter to

USA Springs, informing them of the passing of the ordinance, and stating that their business plan was in violation of local law.

USA Springs stopped building when the ordinance passed, and soon after filed for bankruptcy. The Tea Party kept up pressure on the members of the select board by reminding them of their duty to enforce the ordinance. They were also not afraid to remind members of the select board of Article 8 of the New Hampshire Constitution, which states that it is the duty of elected officials to execute the will of the people, and if they don't, they may be removed.

> OLIVIA ZINK: Now I can share with other people that this is what the residents of New Hampshire are doing to take back their water supply. It may seem strange to say, but I hope the ordinance gets challenged because it will present an opportunity, a tool to spread the message wider.

Gail Darrell also reflected on her involvement with getting the ordinance passed:

> People say: "You passed the ordinance in Barnstead? How did you do that?" I tell them you have to be willing to take the time to talk to people, lots of people, about what you see as the problem. It takes perseverance, a person who's committed, and who doesn't give up. To be effective, you have to learn from what you do and keep going, and you have to keep the faith and the hope, because these fights are long and there are many losses along the way. But how else am I going to answer to my children?

Chapter 3

GIVING NATURE THE RIGHT TO EXIST

Lessons Learned

- *In order to protect your local environment, you must first change your way of thinking about nature. Recognize that it has the right to exist and to flourish.*

- *It's important to have a support group, because the fight is often long and hard, and persistence is key. Standing up to a corporation may mean facing the threat of being sued.*

- *Networking is crucial with others inside the community as well as those outside it. Realizing that others share your struggle provides strength.*

In nature, one creature's waste is often recycled as another's food. Increasingly, human waste has become a toxic mix of the by-products of commercial and industrial production. This has had serious consequences for the environment. Many of us still hold to the notion that we can "throw things away" without realizing that a place "away" from everything else never did exist. More often than not, throwing something away these days means dumping it in someone else's community—usually a poor community, either urban or rural, where people don't have the clout to fight these practices.

Tamaqua Borough in Pennsylvania is one such place. After years of absorbing egregious amounts of toxic waste, Tamaqua grew tired of trying to get environmental protection laws to work for them. A sick environment will create sick people, so it's no coincidence that a local nurse banded together with a patient and a doctor to try a new way of getting governmental action.

They recognized that they would never find protection under the current structure of law, which treats natural communities and ecosystems as property, intended for human use, profit, and exploitation.

Because they had come to recognize that their lives were not separate from nature, but instead profoundly interdependent, the people in Tamaqua sought to have their local laws reflect this new understanding. This meant they would have to discard the old notion of "environmental protection" and instead learn to think of ecosystems as having their own inalienable rights.

The borough council members and the mayor struggled to come to agreement about this innovative law. As in many other communities, some representatives were determined to try something new on behalf of their constituents, while others balked at the possibility of being sued by companies whose activities might be banned or by state officials beholden to such companies. The people of Tamaqua had to realize that as long as they were operating in fear of such an eventuality, they were not free to decide what was best for their own community. They decided to cast off that fear.

Sludge Dumping Threatens Tamaqua

Tamaqua is a borough of about seven thousand people one hundred miles west of Philadelphia, in eastern Schuylkill County. According to its residents, Tamaqua is a Native American name for "running water," although others say it means "land of the beaver." On certain days the rivers that run through town turn an oily yellow-orange from the toxic runoff of old coal mines. No beavers have been sighted near these waters for years.

Tamaqua is situated within the Pennsylvania coal region of the Appalachian Mountains. Coal mining was an extremely vital economic activity in the region throughout the twentieth century, but it has since experienced a decline. What remains are gigantic pits, in some cases twice the size of nearby towns.

Over the past few years, pit owners have been able to turn a profit by inviting companies outside the state to use their sites as dumping grounds for industrial and wastewater sludge. Euphemistically called "biosolids," sludge contains a number of toxic substances, which leach into local aquifers, rivers, and reservoirs.

In Tamaqua, there are no protections offered against leaching. The runoff goes into the rivers and creeks that run by the homes of Tamaqua to join the Little Schuylkill River, which feeds the larger Schuylkill, which then goes on to supply the city of Philadelphia. During a series of hearings with the Department of Environmental Protection, residents were given the opportunity to ask questions about the process of sludge dumping. During one of these sessions, they discovered that the Lehigh Coal and Navigation Company planned to start filling old mine pits not only with sludge, but also with fly ash—a fine, powdery substance generated in the combustion of coal. This process would turn Tamaqua's old mine pits into unlined landfills for toxic waste and coat the town with poisonous dust.

Department of Environmental Protection officials made public statements to the effect that biosolids and fly ash are not harmful to the environment, and that Tamaqua should feel grateful for the local income, as Lehigh Coal was offering the borough a dollar for every ton of fly ash dumped. The residents of Tamaqua and surrounding boroughs were not easily persuaded. They had already put up with years of government indifference to the rising incidence of disease in their township associated with environmental pollution.

Tamaqua Targeted in the Past

Cathy Miorelli is a registered nurse who works at the local public high school. She and her husband were both born in Tamaqua.

She knows all too well that her community is a hotbed of toxic exposure. Within miles of Tamaqua are three toxic Superfund sites—McAdoo Associates, the Tonolli Corporation, and Eastern Diversified Metals. The area is also home to a number of industrial facilities, including a handful of waste-coal-burning power plants.

Over the years, Miorelli became increasingly aware of the number of recurring illnesses among students at the high school, as well as the high incidence of various cancers, thyroid problems, and multiple sclerosis in the community. Stonewalled by the state's department of health and the Department of Environmental Protection, she decided to run for the local council. After she was elected, she explained her foray into politics:

> I have always been concerned about those that don't have a voice. I got involved for fear of my own children and their safety, wanting the air and water to be safe for them and all the children in school. I ran for office because I wasn't happy with what was being done, or not being done, and too many officials just wanted to take care of their friends.

Through Dr. Peter Baddick, who practices internal medicine in nearby Carbon County, Miorelli met longtime county resident Joe Murphy, who was diagnosed with multiple sclerosis a few years ago. Murphy's family has lived in the borough for five generations. He is articulate and well informed. After being diagnosed, he did some research and discovered that Tamaqua has a much higher rate of multiple sclerosis and cancer than the national average. Why, he wondered, was Tamaqua experiencing such elevated illness levels?

Murphy eventually found out that, along with its well-known Superfund sites, the area has long been a notorious site for illegal "midnight dumpers" unloading toxic waste. Among the volatile by-products in the soil are arsenic, lead, cadmium, zinc, chromium, manganese, trichloroethylene, mercury, PCBs, and vinyl chloride. These chemicals were being remediated with other chemicals, such as lye, and covered up with a coating of earth and grass.

Murphy and Baddick had spent years talking to the Department of Health and the Department of Environmental Protection, alerting them to the high incidence of cancer and other diseases in the borough. They were told there was no way the area could have been contaminated.

When they finally got through to an epidemiologist, they were told their analysis had been correct all along, and that the government agencies were not correctly analyzing their own statistics.

Murphy took a jaded look at the experience: "There's no brass ring to come out and investigate—only to facilitate the bureaucracy.

People think these departments are doing their job of protecting us, but it's not the case."

Miorelli and Murphy came together, thinking that if they could demonstrate that the local cancer cluster was linked to toxic contamination, perhaps they could at least stop the current dumping. They instead found members of the town planning board happy to take the word of various state agencies and corporate officials. For a short time, Lehigh Coal had been forced to stop dumping due to permit violations and nonpayment of back taxes, but the Department of Environmental Protection decided to pay for the company's tax bill and then grant it a new permit. Miorelli could see the corruption happening right in front of her. It was clear that conventional methods were not going to help.

Contact with CELDF

As part of her council member activities, Miorelli attended a meeting in another town where an activist named Ben Price spoke. Price worked in the corporate world as a manager in a trucking company before taking on full-time work as a Democracy School teacher and member of CELDF.

> BEN PRICE: The work is endless and the days off are few, but I'm happier doing this than [my other] job. It has transformed my outlook on life. And the best thing is when I meet someone like Cathy Miorelli, someone willing to take a stand.

Through Price, Cathy Miorelli met Antoinette and Russell Pennock, whose son Daniel died after being exposed to toxic sludge, which had been dumped on the farmland next door to their home. For Miorelli, the couple's grief made the stakes crystal clear. Impressed with Price's broad knowledge about sludge dumping in Pennsylvania communities, as well as his dedication to providing alternative strategies for fighting the practice, Miorelli decided to attend Democracy School.

Democracy School

The Democracy School was held in an adjacent township, and was attended by supervisors from many communities that were struggling with sludge dumping. Miorelli was the only person at the school from Tamaqua. She was completely energized by the experience. Afterward, she was motivated to encourage Tamaqua to be in the forefront of the fight against sludge dumping.

> CATHY MIORELLI: After the Democracy School, I was permanently changed. Most importantly, I learned that we have rights as a local government. I realized that we could act on what we wanted most and put together an ordinance that would prevent contaminants from coming into our town.

Miorelli also learned, however, that all existing environmental laws in the United States are anchored in the concept of nature as property, and were passed under the authority of the United States Constitution's "commerce clause." She was reminded that not so long ago in our country, people were property too. Thomas Linzey explains:

> Until slavery was abolished, a slave master could not be punished for whipping a slave, because that slave was his property, and he had the right to damage it. Until 1920, rape was "property damage." The suffragists and the abolitionists were running up against a structure of law that would not allow them to make the changes they needed. Under our constitution, you're either a person or you're property. What movements do is move and transform that. We won't have a real environmental movement in this country until we realize that nature has rights.

For Miorelli, providing rights to nature seemed self-evident. As she started sharing her new views, her excitement encouraged a few of her colleagues and fellow activists to hold a Democracy School in Tamaqua. With help from CELDF, the group drafted an ordinance banning the dumping of sludge. In Tamaqua, an ordinance must first be proposed and advertised before it can be voted on by the town council. Leading this effort alongside Miorelli was the mayor of Tamaqua Borough, Chris Morrison, who realized in his meetings with state legislators that the sludge industry's billion-dollar profits and lobby carried more weight than the health concerns of a small group of people.

CHRIS MORRISON: Tamaqua is where I am going to stay and create my future. Our biggest issue is taking care of the environment, and I have brought it to the forefront in my tenure as mayor.

The citizens of Tamaqua wanted their local laws to recognize that natural communities and ecosystems possess a fundamental right to exist and flourish, and that residents of those communities possess the legal authority to enforce those rights on behalf of the ecosystem.

As Morrison, Miorelli, and others distributed information leaflets door to door, they were able to make personal contact with people; this was a hugely important organizing tool to garner the

Tamaqua Ordinance

An ordinance to protect the health, safety, and general welfare of the citizens and environment of Tamaqua Borough by banning corporations from engaging in the land application of sewage sludge, by banning persons from using corporations to engage in land application of sewage sludge, by providing for the testing of sewage sludge prior to land application in the borough, by removing constitutional powers of corporations within the borough, by recognizing and enforcing the rights of residents to defend natural communities' ecosystems.

necessary support. Local newspapers also gave the ordinance some positive coverage, which is not usually the case.

Obstacles

As Miorelli and others worked to organize support, one constant obstacle they encountered was that people were so busy they wouldn't take the time to get educated. It was much easier for them to believe that the government would keep them safe rather than finding out for themselves what these pollutants had the potential to do.

Unfortunately, it's only when people are directly threatened that they seem to get motivated, so the task of organizers was to make the dangers to the community more tangible.

The rights for nature spelled out in the ordinance also proved a contentious issue. Opponents felt that rights should not be given to something that isn't "alive and/or not a person." Proponents affirmed that, just as children don't have full legal rights but still deserve to be protected, so, too, should nature be protected. They also pointed out that the ordinance would not stop the free use of private property except where such use interfered with the existence and vitality of the ecosystem.

Eliminating the authority of a property owner to destroy the ecosystem would be far more

effective than trying to regulate how much harm an ecosystem could sustain.

Miorelli also faced an uphill battle with her fellow council members. A few of them liked the dollar-a-ton deal offered by Lehigh Coal, and they believed the statements released by the Department of Energy stating that the dumping was safe. Some council members also had personal associations with various coal companies.

But perhaps the most daunting obstacle to the township passing a challenging form of legislation was the threat of being sued. The Tamaqua solicitor, who saw the purpose of his job as keeping the town council safe from potential lawsuits, spoke strongly against passing the ordinance. He warned that it could be interpreted as challenging state law. Such warnings often end up giving corporations even more power, as the threat of a lawsuit often discourages citizens from enacting measures to curtail corporate activity. It isn't only the township that can be sued, but also the individual members of the town council. Each member of the council has to face down this threat in their own way.

Mayor Chris Morrison's response was clear: "If I am going to be sued, so be it. You want to take my row home, my little car, good luck, you can have them. We are going to protect our community."

Miorelli knew that the Tamaqua council vote would probably be split, so she managed to get a large crowd to attend the council meeting in order to put pressure on the representatives. At the meeting, she read aloud a portion of the Pennsylvania State Constitution that specifically acknowledges local control.

The mayor cast the deciding vote, and the borough of Tamaqua passed the anti-sludge ordinance, becoming the first community in the United States to provide rights to nature.

Tamaqua Passes a Second Ordinance

Following the success of the ordinance, the borough council passed a second ordinance the following spring banning anything else the waste corporations might want to haul in. At one of the many public meetings, a representative from the Department of Environmental Protection came to defend the dumping permits. She declared there was no evidence of fly ash being unsafe. Before a crowded room of over a hundred citizens, the mayor confronted her.

CHRIS MORRISON: I asked her if she would like to put a teaspoon of fly ash in her water glass and mix it up

Tamaqua Ordinance

Section 6.6: It shall be unlawful for any corporation or its directors, officers, owners, or managers to interfere with the existence and flourishing of natural communities or ecosystems, or to cause damage to those natural communities and ecosystems.

and drink it. She said, "Absolutely not." I then said, "You won't drink it, but it's okay for us to breathe it?"

Enforcement

Despite the new ordinances, coal companies still intended to fill up the community's mine pits with fly ash. When the council received a letter from the Department of Environmental Protection telling them that permits had indeed been granted to dump fly ash in the borough, the council responded with a letter containing their ordinance and stating that they would enforce it.

The Tamaqua ordinances state that if the borough doesn't enforce the sludge ban, individuals in the community are authorized to do so themselves. Should the case arise that local enforcement officers are negligent in enforcing the ordinances, Miorelli and others are ready to do so. CELDF has promised free legal assistance when and if the time comes for them to act.

Democracy Spreads to Other Townships

A few months after the ordinance passed in Tamaqua, Cathy Miorelli learned that thirty-three dump-truck loads of New Jersey sewage sludge had been dumped on a field about seventy-five yards from the Still Creek Reservoir, which lies in Packer Township, Carbon County, and provides drinking water for Tamaqua and other communities. At first, the Department of Environmental Protection claimed there was no record of sludge being dumped, and that they couldn't find any permits. But like all good activists, Miorelli was nothing if not persistent. In response to more pressure, a representative from the Department of Environmental Protection said it was "lime" that had been dumped by the reservoir, not sludge. He then corrected himself after Miorelli sent him photos of the dump site. She also succeeded in getting local media to print stories, letters, and an editorial that put a spotlight on Packer Township. Then she talked to Tom Gerhart, Chair of the Packer Township Board of Supervisors, and told him about the Tamaqua ordinance.

It took six months until the Packer Township supervisors, impressed with what they were learning, made a motion to advertise a meeting to discuss an ordinance to ban dumping. A number of informational public meetings followed, and flyers explaining the ordinance were distributed. The Packer solicitor, who had worked with the solicitor from Tamaqua, urged the supervisors not to "make a bad move" and expose themselves to the risk of being sued. At the voting meeting, the room was filled to capacity. Gerhart thought that when it came down to the three supervisors voting, one would certainly oppose. Before the vote, this supervisor asked the crowd for a show of hands in favor of the ordinance. Because of the overwhelming support, he too voted to pass the ordinance. After the unanimous vote, the entire room gave the supervisors a standing ovation.

Packer Township Kicks It up a Notch

There was, however, a quick reaction from the state. Officials from the attorney general's office asked to meet privately with the township supervisors. Reaction from the supervisors was swift and unequivocal. They voted in an amendment to the ordinance that they would not meet with anyone from the attorney general's office.

> TOM GERHART: We will not meet behind closed doors, behind the backs of our residents. We are standing our ground and we will take our chances.

CELDF has volunteered to represent the township at no cost should there be a lawsuit.

After sending this letter, the Packer Board did indeed vote to revoke the attorney general's "authority to enforce undemocratic law that nullifies community rights." They committed into the township's legal framework a new ordinance to not "surrender community members' rights to the state, which purports to have empowered its top law-enforcement officer to act as private litigator for the waste-hauling industry." By adopting this amendment, the members of the board of supervisors honored their obligation to act on behalf of the people in their community, and to protect the health, safety, and welfare of the people and environment in which they live.

An Open Letter to the Office of the Attorney General of Pennsylvania

From the Board of Township Supervisors,
Packer Township, Carbon County

Dear Attorney General Corbett,

The people of Packer Township are in receipt of your letter. In it, the office of the Attorney General informs us that Packer Township resident Mr. Clyde Hinkle requested your office "review" the Packer Township Local Control, Sewage Sludge and Chemical Trespass Ordinance.

According to your letter to us, "[Act 38] authorizes the Office, in its discretion, to file a lawsuit against the municipality if, upon review, the Office believes that the ordinance unlawfully limits or restricts a normal agricultural operation." We write to inform you that the Ordinance was adopted with majority support of the people within Packer Township, via the Township Supervisors, and that therefore, the Ordinance will not be rescinded, and that we will not negotiate away any portion of it.

The ACRE law was drafted and adopted by agribusiness corporate interests, using the legislature as a vehicle, and was not passed to aid family farmers, but agribusiness interests. It is an undemocratic and illegitimate law under a system in which the consent of the people directly affected by such governing decisions is made irrelevant. The Attorney General's office is administering an illegitimate and therefore unconstitutional law, and we refuse to recognize its enforceability.

If the Attorney General's office pursues this matter, please be aware that the Township is reviewing for adoption an amendment to the Ordinance that refuses to recognize that the Attorney General has any jurisdiction within this municipality to enforce a law which runs so contrary to democratic principles.

Additionally, should you determine it to be a matter of state interest to attempt to use the courts to deprive the people of Packer Township of their rights, including a right to self-government, and a healthy environment, any offer to meet with the elected representatives of this community to "negotiate" a voluntary surrender of those rights will be rejected.

Sincerely,
Packer Township Board of Supervisors,
RR 1, Weatherly, PA 18255

4

TRUE DEMOCRACY: AN ONGOING CONVERSATION

Lessons Learned

• *Build coalitions to develop a comprehensive vision for the community.*

• *Learn to solve differences of opinion through conversation and by developing relationships.*

• *Work to translate the new community vision into a city charter.*

I n smaller communities, organizing often begins in reaction to a specific threat; in a large community, residents usually have a host of concerns that need to be addressed in order to create a vision for the city as a whole. One possible and very effective way to translate this vision into reality is to mount a campaign to add a bill of rights to the city charter. Forty-three states currently have "home rule" statutes or constitutional provisions that allow for a city to adopt a charter or to amend one already in existence.

The ensuing citywide conversation will involve various groups coming together to decide first the rights agreed on by all, and then to define the language that best expresses those rights. This process can be both painstaking and exciting, and it starts with good community organizers who know how to get the conversation going. Democracy in action can get rowdy and contentious at times, and it demands of us commitment and a deep faith in ourselves and in each other.

Spokane and Its Residents' Concerns

Spokane is the metropolitan center of the Inland Northwest, located on the Spokane River in eastern Washington. It's a classic American city with about two hundred thousand people living in the city proper and about half a million in the surrounding county. The natural world is in abundance here, and has long attracted outdoor sports enthusiasts and tourists. The Spokane metropolitan area has seen an influx of new residents in recent years, and the downtown area has undergone a major rebirth, attracting the development of over five hundred projects worth over two billion dollars. The Spokane River runs through downtown in a series of mighty falls that give the town its characteristic beauty. Once a major area for salmon fishing and a natural gathering place for dozens of Northwest native tribes, the river is now one of the most polluted in the country.

The city of Spokane covers an area of 58.5 square miles. Its population is largely white. About 11 percent of the population lives below the poverty line. Virtually every social class is represented in Spokane's twenty-seven neighborhoods, many of which are of such charm and character that they are recognized on the

National Register of Historical Districts. Each of these neighborhoods has its own citizen council that meets regularly to discuss pressing issues. An assembly of these councils makes recommendations to the city government. Two of the pressing issues for many neighborhoods are adequate housing and overdevelopment.

Neighborhoods and Development

In Spokane, as in a number of other places, developers and neighborhood communities are often at odds about specific projects proposed. For example, one developer wanted to build a high-rise condominium on a hill overlooking a quaint, relatively low-income neighborhood called Peaceful Valley. The people in the neighborhood objected, as the building would tower over their homes and block out light, clog limited road access, and destroy the old-growth pines on the hillside below where the development was planned. Against all objections, the city government went ahead and approved a building permit for the condo development.

Lori Aluna, Sally Combelic, and Patty Norton—members of the Peaceful Valley neighborhood council—voiced their frustration in running up against the structure of power. The reality is that the councils have no real power because members of the city government do not have to follow any of the suggestions made to them.

> LORI ALUNA: We need a different way of governing
> that isn't the people with power and money influencing

the other people with power and money and controlling everyone else.

These women have demonstrated a rare persistence, in part due to a driving sense of justice. They are outraged that the developers say things like, "Well, just sell your house if you don't like what we're doing." These women do not consider their houses as assets, but as homes. Indeed, they share a deep love for and commitment to their little neighborhood. They won a small victory when the city appeals process sided with them. But when the developer threatened the city with a lawsuit, the ruling was overturned. They are dreading the day construction starts. Aluna voices the thoughts of many residents:

> Why are the trees on the slope considered expendable? Until we stop seeing the planet as a resource that is ours to consume instead of the place that supports our life, we're heading toward our own extinction. Why can't we make a little less money, build affordable housing and leave the trees?

In another area of town, residents of the Southgate neighborhood objected when a corporation put in an application to build three big-box stores. The residents opposed the plan—claiming it would destroy the area's natural environment and create a huge infrastructure problem for the neighborhood—and appealed to the city council. They brought in planning and environmental experts to speak on their behalf.

Brad Read, a popular high-school teacher as well as a longtime activist, served on the Spokane City Human Rights Commission for five years. He went to the big-box hearing in the city council chambers, and he said that what he saw felt like the movie *Groundhog Day*. The neighborhood presented its case in front of the hearing examiner and the experts testified. When they got done, the city planner and the representative of the development corporation got up and informed the hearing examiner that, by law, he was bound to ignore virtually all of the testimony presented by the neighborhood group because the only person who had legal standing was the woman who lived next door to one of the parcels of land in question. Then the appeal permit was granted. The neighborhood residents were clearly not the constituency being served under this law.

> BRAD READ: The neighbors had done the hard work of local democracy by gathering to defend their community against an unwanted assault, and they were told by the structure of law and governance that their views and concerns didn't matter.

In both of the above situations, while the law governing development recognized the rights of the development corporation, it did not

recognize that the neighborhood had any rights to reject the development.

These communities learned that the law endows corporations with constitutional "rights" that are automatically violated when a neighborhood attempts to stop a project. Thus, neighborhoods are almost always on the losing end of any decision. While the city of Spokane has a process in place for exercising local control, in reality, citizens don't have the ability to exercise such control.

Work and Unions

Separately, the big-box stores raised other issues of concern. Along with chain stores and fast-food restaurants, big-box stores often drive smaller, locally owned businesses out of business, creating economic dislocation and despair. The jobs they offer tend to be low wage and without benefits. Company owners use many tactics, such as the threat of job loss, to stall and oppose labor organizing. Unions in Spokane have long been working toward unionization for employees of the big-box stores, but without much success. Constitutional rights such as the right to privacy, free speech, and assembly, as well as due process, have never existed in the private workplace. The lack of these constitutional protections makes it difficult for members of labor unions to take action to improve wages and work environment.

The Spokane River

The state of the Spokane River is of huge concern to many citizens. A number of manufacturing companies have located in the area, drawn by the easy access to raw materials and cheap hydroelectric power provided by dams in the neighboring state of Idaho. While Spokane's residents welcome business and the jobs it arguably brings, they worry about how much pollution the air and especially the river can sustain. Some studies show that there are 90 percent fewer fish in the river than there used to be, and that toxic chemicals in the river leach into aquifers, endangering the region's source of clean water. People are warned not to eat fish from the river, and the rate of contamination in breast milk is high.

Inadequate regulation and poor enforcement allow factories to pour toxins into the waters to such a degree that some scientists have compared the river to a terminally ill patient.

Shallan Dawson, a member of the Sierra Club's executive committee, is striving to protect the river she loves. According to Dawson, the Environmental Protection Agency considers toxic waste dumped into the river from upstream Idaho to be "natural background" rather than pollution. Adding insult to injury, the citizens of Spokane are also dealing with phosphorus from local wastewater treatment plants being discharged into the river, causing heavy pollution.

> SHALLAN DAWSON: It's so frustrating that the state's Department of Environmental Quality is ignoring its own studies and not enforcing the laws on the books.

In addition, during the summer months, to the chagrin of many local residents, the river gets "turned off" by dams upstream. This may add to the enjoyment of those who live on the lake upriver, and it may increase revenue from power production, but when the dam is opened up in the fall, tons of suspended toxins and heavy metals rush downstream. Federal agencies routinely preempt local control over related environmental issues. Recently, the Federal Regulatory Commission held hearings on the relicensing of dams owned by the energy company Avista. Afterward, public discussion regarding the use of the dams was closed, by law, for fifty years.

Reframing the Problems in Democracy School

Breean Beggs is the director of the Center for Justice, a local nonprofit law firm working to promote social justice for the citizens of Spokane. He and Jim Sheehan, who is the founder of the center, had the opportunity to hear Thomas Linzey speak, and they invited him to teach Democracy School in their city.

JIM SHEEHAN: Our conversation had long revolved around the question: How do we make this place more democratic? Everyone has a voice, but do they have a forum, and how do we get a forum for people to be heard?

They were captivated by this new way of dealing with corporate powers, which teaches everyday citizens how to determine their own destiny through conversation and open decision-making. Word of the school spread, and leaders from the neighborhood councils attended, as well as others who cared about Spokane.

BREEAN BEGGS: Democracy School taught me the history I didn't learn in law school. Corporate entities are meant to provide a public service, and, after the founding of our country, they were tightly controlled. They were meant to be tools of society, not considered as natural-born persons.

Another attendee was Brad Read, who had spent a lot of energy trying to get the city council to pass a number of nonbinding resolutions. At a certain point, he realized that these resolutions might make people feel good but were not enforceable law, and were therefore ultimately meaningless. The school showed him why they needed enforceable law.

BRAD READ: I realized we've all gone through the same process with our organizing, which was about asking nicely and being denied, and realizing we don't have control.

Shallan Dawson found the school unsettling. It made her realize how much of her work with the Sierra Club had been essentially ineffective. At a recent meeting of the Sierra Club, the Environmental Protection Agency had agreed that the way water-discharge permits for the Spokane River were formulated did not count toxic discharge from other states. But before the environmentalists could celebrate this decision, they learned that although new draft permits would soon go into effect, offending companies would be given ten additional years to meet the new standards. Dawson realized that company stakeholders had more rights than the people of Spokane.

> SHALLAN DAWSON: I came to environmental protection with total idealism. I went to work doing river protection, being sure we would succeed, because people care, and they are willing to write letters and work harder and harder. But until you have enforceable law on the books, you won't see real improvement in water quality.

In Spokane, Democracy School did three things. First, it validated the idea that working through the regulatory system is a waste of time, as Dawson and others had clearly experienced. Second, it empowered individuals to realize they could create the community they wanted. As Patty Norton from Peaceful Valley observed: "It's hard to change the conversation from 'what can we get' to 'what do we want?' We've been so beaten down, we were only focused on what little concessions we could get. Democracy School helps you change that conversation."

Finally, it demonstrated that individual rights at the local level are the most powerful tools for change available.

As more schools were taught in the area, the community spirit became infectious; attendees began getting together to discuss what could be done in their city.

Out of these many conversations, Envision Spokane was born. The group quickly attracted a lot of people, including representatives from Spokane's neighborhood associations, community groups, churches, and labor unions, to discuss what they wanted for their city. While it started out as an envisioning exercise, the work transformed into a citywide campaign to rewrite Spokane's Home Rule Charter—to drive legally enforceable rights for neighborhoods, people, and nature directly into the structure of the city government itself. Envision Spokane asked CELDF to help them explore how this could be done.

Researching Spokane's Governing Structures

The city of Spokane makes decisions through a mayor-council form of government. Interestingly, it is also a "home-rule city," which makes it attractive as a place for rights-based organizing. Municipal home rule began in the early twentieth century. Stimulated by what was called the progressive movement—which came into existence in response to government corruption and waste, and pushed reforms to give citizens more power over their own lives—it gave local citizens the right to adopt a charter for the community allowing them fundamental governing powers over local issues. Of course, under our present legal system, home rule can be trumped by state and federal laws.

> BREEAN BEGGS: In the city charter, you have two opportunities to shift the balance: We can identify and expand the rights individuals have, and we can take back certain rights that have been granted to corporations.

The goal and aim of Envision Spokane is to literally rewrite the charter of the city by putting on the ballot a number of amendments for voters to consider.

Local Organizing Clusters

One challenge that arises in the process of organizing a city, as opposed to a small rural community, is the complexity and variety of interests presented by citizens. How do you create the possibility for so many different people to have input in the process? How do those already involved encourage a large amount of participation, so that they are representing everyone's concerns, yet also keep the process manageable? How do you realize a far-reaching intention that will require conversations numbering in the thousands?

The Envision Spokane participants, after establishing a permanent board, addressed this challenge by deciding to divide their members into three clusters: the neighborhood council cluster, the labor union cluster, and the community group cluster. The community group cluster included social justice advocacy, environmental organizations, and independent organizations such as business groups. Each cluster was invited to gather more participants to meet and discuss their vision for a bill of rights for the city of Spokane. This process was similarly painstaking and enlightening for each cluster, although different in particulars.

For Rick Evans of Labor Local #2389, who grew up in Spokane, the process was different from how he usually proceeds in his organizing: "We were being asked to make a wish list of what we would want as part of the Spokane charter. Normally we do top-down stuff like talking to owners of a company or setting up a picket line where job conditions are wrong. But working with Envision Spokane is more in tune with building coalitions."

The labor union cluster went through a process of prioritizing. Evans concluded that their final three proposed amendments reflected the make-up of those who were present the most.

That's how the democratic process works—you have to speak up if you want your voice to be heard. Nevertheless, as various unions were in discussion with each other during the negotiations, the amendments do represent the majority of common labor concerns. The cluster agreed on the right to be paid a living wage, the right to be paid the prevailing wage on construction projects, and the right to have constitutional protections within the workplace.

A consensus also began emerging in the neighborhood council cluster. The members prioritized seven concrete amendments all could agree on, although hammering out the precise language required a fair amount of effort. Rather than claiming the right to veto development projects, the group settled on the more general "right to determine their own futures." The group also determined it had the right for growth-related infrastructure costs to be provided by any new construction developments.

The community group cluster presented a wider array of concerns, including business-related issues, health care and housing issues, and questions about the environment. There was strong interest in providing greater rights to small businesses, which often have trouble accessing loans. To meet the goal of a sustainable city, it makes sense to find systemic ways to support local business so that the town is not dependent on national franchises, which don't have the same investment in the community.

Protecting the Spokane River from further damage was another thing easily agreed upon by everyone in the cluster. Participants followed the CELDF model and created an amendment to give nature a right to exist and to flourish. Their thinking was: If the Spokane River has rights, then individuals can speak on its behalf in order to protect it.

> BREEAN BEGGS: We're a swing city politically, but everybody loves the river. As people have conversations about what they want to pass on to their grandchildren, they find common ground.

Mariah McKay, an articulate young activist, served as secretary to the community group cluster. She urged using the Internet to get the word out as well as looking at other ways to get young people involved. She set up a Web site for Envision Spokane and did outreach through Facebook and various Gmail lists.

> MARIAH MCKAY: Developing and printing a flyer is expensive and laborious. We send out Envision Spokane meeting information with a Google alert. Organizing is like art. I would like Spokane to surprise everyone. The point is to enable ourselves to protect and secure the kind of lifestyle and future and environment that we want to be living in.

As it became clearer what the participants of each cluster wanted, the challenge became taking all those ideas and

Spokane Bill of Rights

Residents have the right to a healthy, locally based economy.

Residents have the right to preventive health care.

Residents have the right to housing.

Residents have the right to a healthy environment.

The natural environment has the right to exist and flourish.

Neighborhoods have the right to determine their own futures.

Neighborhoods have the right to have growth-related infrastructure costs provided by new development.

Workers have the right to be paid a living wage, and if greater, to be paid the prevailing wage on construction projects.

Workers have the right to employer neutrality when unionizing and the right to constitutional protections within the workplace.

Workers have the right to work as apprentices on construction projects.

Residents, neighborhoods, workers, neighborhood councils, and the City of Spokane have the right to enforce these charter amendments.

condensing them into to a reasonable set of proposals that could gain wide support and be voted into the city's charter.

Brad Read exuded great enthusiasm for the project: "This organizing is radically new. We are actually writing law, which is something this community has never undertaken before."

Should the city vote to pass the amendments, the Center for Justice has offered its legal staff to help enforce whatever rights Spokane has decided to place in its governing charter.

Permanent Board Selects Charter Amendments

When the three clusters came back together as the Envision Spokane board, there were twenty-one proposed amendments between them. They realized that this number was too unwieldy to win approval by the general electorate. Each amendment was presented to the group in a briefing paper and then voted on to rank the top three from each cluster. Where there was clear overlap, the group was able to sign off relatively easily. The board ultimately agreed upon eleven proposals to constitute a bill of rights for the city charter, although the process of reconsidering and refining continued for another six months.

What They Learned

The process of coming together and hashing out the amendments for the final bill of rights was a truly rewarding experience for many participants. Of course, there were differences among each cluster's wishes. It would have been natural for the conflict to become heated as various parties pushed for the amendments they considered most crucial.

Everyone found that talking to each other and developing relationships not only circumnavigated this potential problem, but also turned out to be the greatest part of the process.

Members often found themselves unwilling to stop their meeting at the appointed time and would still be there hours later, hashing out language and concepts.

> LOIS IRWIN: We were all happy to meet others coming from different walks of life. We developed a sense of loyalty to one another and we learned from one another. These are the only meetings I've attended where I left feeling better than when I arrived.

Members of the board reported growing satisfaction as they got to know people from their city they didn't normally have the opportunity to meet. They were able to come to a deeper understanding of their fellow citizens and the issues they faced, and to learn more about the place they all inhabit.

Obstacles

As in many other cities, a few small groups have most of the power in Spokane. A major business family also owns a city newspaper, which means that major media will not necessarily be on the side of Envision Spokane. The Spokane utility corporation effectively owns the Spokane River. The organizers of Envision Spokane expect a strong pushback from these and other entrenched powers, anticipating that their efforts will be made to look silly, ridiculous, and even dangerous. To counteract this, they have spread word of their message throughout the Web, and were recently pleased by the publication of a positive article in a weekly paper calling the group "cheerful rebels."

Another obstacle that activists face is citizen apathy. Many people believe that those in power will come up with solutions to their problems. As well, many people are busy with their own lives and families, struggling to get by; for these people, participation in the larger life of the community may be overwhelming. Nor have all of Spokane's residents had the unusual opportunity to get together and discuss their opinions and issues. But the town hall process will offer the chance for proposals to be presented to large audiences throughout the city. This will allow the new proposals to be modified as an increasing number of Spokane residents have their voices heard. Some of these meetings may be contentious, as, for example, some members of the chamber of commerce may not agree with the notion that local neighborhoods should be provided with the power to stop new development. But such is the process required of a true democracy.

What is so compelling to those in Envision Spokane doing all the hard work is that, if their proposals pass, their amendments will become law. It will then be the responsibility of the city to enforce the provisions and remedy any of these new rights if they are violated.

Brad Read is excited for that day to come:

> It feels new because we don't usually focus on the part of our history where the abolitionists and suffragists changed illegitimate law. The only way they could do this was by doing the educational work it took to build a big enough movement.

The fundamental truth is deciding about who's in charge. When it comes to the decisions that affect your community and your children, and what the common future is going to look like, who gets to decide?

If it's you, congratulations, you have democracy. If not, what are you going to do about it?

Chapter 5

MEETING NEW CHALLENGES

Lessons Learned

- *New problems require new solutions. What works in one locality may not work for another. Even innovation needs to keep evolving.*

- *Use the energy of a large group to push for change.*

- *If your current government isn't working to protect your community, don't be afraid to create a new governmental framework.*

As the energy crisis intensifies, communities all across the country will come face to face with mining companies who want to extract resources from the earth. The projects proposed will be harmful to local environments and local economies. In the fight against fossil-fuel lobbies, citizens will most likely not be able to depend on their elected state and local governments to protect their interests, as billions of dollars will be at stake. Nuclear power will increasingly be promoted as a partial solution to the energy crisis. Mining corporations, especially those that mine uranium, will look to build new projects east of the Mississippi, where such mining has never occurred before.

Unlike New Hampshire, with its strong local democratic structure, and the states of Pennsylvania and Washington, which give citizens some decision-making power through the home-rule process, Virginia's residents do not have such legal recourses. The organizing in Virginia therefore has to be even more innovative—people will have to create it as they go along. But while corporations have money and lobbyists on their side, the community has the energy that comes from fighting for a just cause. The concerned citizens of Virginia are learning that it is their conviction and ability to get a large, passionate group involved that is making the difference in getting the results they need.

Environmental Assault Threatens Community

Halifax is a small town in Halifax County, with a population of just under 1,400. It lies southeast of Pittsylvania County, the largest county in Virginia, in the region known as Southside—a cluster of nine counties sitting on the North Carolina border. Known for its gently rolling hills, beautiful historic towns, and strong sense of tradition, Southside attracts people who are looking for southern hospitality and a sense of community. Economically, it has suffered from losses of tobacco farming and textile jobs, and the increase in prisons in the area has provided the only real source of new employment. The area also happens to be home to what is touted to be the largest undeveloped uranium deposit in the United States.

Group Forms to Fight Assault

In the early 1980s, people in Halifax got wind of plans by Union Carbide and the Canadian Marline Corporation to mine uranium in their community. They formed a group called Southside Concerned Citizens in order to prevent such mining. The group organized vigorously throughout the state. In 1982, with the price of uranium falling and no regulatory structure in place, the state legislature voted for a temporary reprieve against mining instead of an outright ban. In 1989, Union Carbide and Marline abandoned their leases.

When uranium prices began to rise again, Virginia Uranium, a corporation that buys up leases, was already engaged in exploratory drilling at the Pittsylvania County site. The corporation expected to make nine billion dollars by mining two thousand acres on Coles Hill, the antebellum estate owned by Walter Coles, who formed the corporation. When the Virginia energy bill was being drafted, Walter Coles' brother-in-law, Secretary of Transportation Whitt Clement, convinced his friends in the Virginia Senate to include an endorsement of possible uranium mining in Pittsylvania County. Even though Walter Coles told community members that he would not mine the land unless it could be done safely, he no longer has control of Virginia Uranium—it is now owned by Canadian corporations. Through the active work of fifteen full-time lobbyists, a regulatory program was approved and the temporary reprieve against mining was overturned.

The citizens of Halifax, which is downwind and downriver from the Pittsylvania mining site, do not want mining to take place.

Their research has convinced them that uranium mining has never been done safely anywhere, and that open-pit uranium mining would devastate the local landscape and contaminate the environment.

They know that other regions have been severely impacted by hard-rock mining, and that their local economy could collapse.

Protecting a Community

Jack Dunavant is the chairman of Southside Concerned Citizens. An engineer, he runs a construction business that employs his two sons and his daughter. His family has lived in Halifax since the 1700s. In the early 1980s, when Southside Concerned Citizens needed someone with expertise, Dunavant stepped up. At first he wondered, "What's the harm in mining for uranium?" but once he delved into what happens in the process, he could not remain ambivalent.

Most people think of the dangers of uranium in terms of its use in nuclear weaponry rather than its relatively more simple removal from the ground. Uranium is found in bedrock. To mine uranium, workers blast bedrock to break it up. This exposes uranium as well as any heavy metals that surround it. This material is brought up to the surface, crushed into fine powder, and then filtered through caustic compounds and acids to leach out 14 to 18 percent of the desired ore. The rest remains in a pile of waste called tailings.

Mine tailings are either combined with water and held in sludge ponds or kept in piles up to twenty stories high. The waste spreads as wind blows the particulates around or rain leaches contaminants into the groundwater. Released into the environment are heavy metals—including arsenic, lead, and mercury—as well as radioactive materials such as thorium-230, radium-22, and radon-222 and its progeny, the radioactive isotopes of bismuth, polonium, and lead. These radioactive contaminants persist in the environment for practically forever. They are bio-accumulative, becoming part of the food chain and causing cancer, leukemia, and genetic mutations in animals and humans. Leached into ground and surface water in Pittsylvania County, they would contaminate the Roanoke River Watershed, which reaches all the way to Virginia Beach, North Carolina's Albemarle Sound, and the Atlantic Ocean.

Uranium mining has usually been done in the arid and sparsely populated areas of the American West. The Southside region of Virginia receives an average of forty-four inches of rain a year. As far as Dunavant is concerned, there's no way that this water can be contained or purified. It will simply percolate through the waste material like water through coffee grounds. The Bannister River flows right by the mine site, and Halifax is the first community downstream, deriving its water directly from the river.

In the 1980s, Dunavant and Southside Concerned Citizens spent countless hours organizing their protest, and Dunavant went to the capital, Richmond, to speak three times. Twenty-five years later, he finds himself in the process of repeating his steps. During the intervening years, as he continued his participation with Southside Concerned Citizens, he also became a member of the Halifax Town Council. Even though he doesn't like politics, he wanted to have a voice politically because, as he states, "that's where the game is played."

The New Threat

When Virginia Uranium came on the scene, it obtained a permit from the Virginia state legislature to proceed with exploratory drilling. The company applied for the permit as the Southside Cattle Company, hoping citizens would not put two and two together. However, since the property is zoned for agricultural use, the company needed a special-use permit, which it did not ask for until after it started drilling. Two hundred and fifty people attended the zoning board meeting, the majority of which were against granting the special-use permit. The zoning board was courageous and refused, in part because Virginia Uranium had already shown disregard for law. Virginia Uranium promptly appealed the decision, and the appeals board granted them the permit.

CELDF Gets Involved

The emerging controversy received statewide media coverage, and Dunavant's name became widely known. He was contacted by Shireen Parsons, a CELDF organizer in Virginia, who told him of CELDF's program of assisting communities to fend off corporate assaults through rights-based organizing and local self-governance. He invited Parsons to present to his group.

> JACK DUNAVANT: I immediately liked the message of going back to constitutional guarantees. We have been trampled too long by big business.

Shireen Parsons has been an activist since moving to Virginia after raising her kids in Washington, D.C. She loves the beauty of the New River Valley. She met Thomas Linzey when he was assisting Montgomery County citizens in their effort to prevent construction of the Smart Road, and she feels honored to have been arrested and thrown in jail with him when they protested the ground-breaking ceremony. Linzey asked Parsons to be on the CELDF board, and she attended the second-ever Democracy School. She was stoked by it, she said, and she felt that she was finally hearing the truth being told. She later became a community organizer for the state of Virginia. Loving what she does and having a healthy sense of humor has helped when Parsons has been accused of being a communist, an outsider, and a troublemaker.

Organizers have to develop a certain toughness and an understanding that moving forward will call up resistance by the forces aligned against change. A good organizer sees this kind of resistance as a positive sign that the job is getting done.

"What we're working to achieve has to happen," says Parsons. "I truly believe it's inevitable."

Halifax Passes the Chemical Trespass Ordinance

The challenge facing the group in Halifax was that the proposed mining was not in their own township, and they had no authority to ban an activity in neighboring Pittsylvania County. They therefore had to think of their ordinance differently, seeking to protect their residents from the deleterious effects of mining happening outside the borders of their township. The group conceived what they called "The Town of Halifax Corporate Mining, Chemical Bodily Trespass, and Community Self-Government Ordinance," the purpose of which is to protect the health, safety, and welfare of the citizens and the environment of Halifax by prohibiting chemical bodily trespass and chemical pollution of their environment, by establishing strict liability for corporate toxic trespass, by removing claims to legal privileges from corporations, and by recognizing and enforcing the rights of residents to defend their rights and by subordinating mining corporations to the people of Halifax.

What this means is that if mining is done and radioactive and chemical contamination occurs in Halifax, both the mining corporation as well as Pittsylvania County, which would have allowed the mining to occur, would be criminally liable for bodily trespass. The town would be required to bring criminal charges against both the corporation and the county, and would have the ability and the responsibility to litigate on behalf of affected citizens. This ordinance counteracts the fact that, up to this point, monitoring and oversight by regulatory agencies has been inadequate to nonexistent. Violations that happen to be discovered or exposed rarely result in penalties, and when they do, they are often a tax-deductible business expense.

As Jack Dunavant read the words of the Chemical Trespass Ordinance, tears came to his eyes.

This is the way this country was set up, what the American Revolution was fought for. Instead of being about how much influence you can buy, it's about the people deciding what happens.

When Southside Concerned Citizens showed community members the ordinance, the conversation often stopped at the part that strips corporations of personhood rights. Many people were concerned that the ordinance would strip their own businesses of all rights. Shireen Parsons explained: "You have the same rights as any other person. And if your business is not harming the community, then your business doesn't need those personhood rights. The fundamental issue is about changing the structure of law to change the structure of power." She observed how often people don't know about the laws that govern them.

People know that the U.S. Constitution's Bill of Rights protects them from the government, but not that corporations are considered private actors. Because corporations have the same rights as individuals, we have no constitutional recourse to damage done to us by corporations.

Gathering Support for the Ordinance

Enough people became concerned about the mining issue that they came to the town council meeting. Parsons spoke on behalf of the ordinance, the council attorney spoke against it, and some of the members of the council, reluctant to pass it, decided to send it to the planning commission. At this point, it was the energy of the group that turned the tide. After Dunavant read aloud portions of the Virginia state constitution, which guarantees certain individual rights, a great number of people at the hearing demanded that it be passed. In spite of their own skepticism, the city council members, conscious of the will of their constituents, passed the ordinance unanimously.

Since then, people are calling the group from all over the country.

JACK DUNAVANT: People are interested in the chemical trespass ordinances for their communities. I tell them you can't go in to your representatives with your hat in your hand and ask please. You have to go in there with an angry crowd.

As Southside Concerned Citizens was well aware, one tiny town saying no was not enough. The goal is for Pittsylvania County itself, where the uranium mine is located, to ban mining. So Southside Concerned Citizens is continuing to fight the battle through local boards and town councils as well as at the state legislature in Richmond. The Coal and Energy Commission, an advisory body, finally sanctioned a two-year study of uranium mining, which gave organizers some breathing room. If the commission were to involve the National Academy of Sciences, and if people were to ask the right questions and receive honest answers, the studies would show why uranium mining must not occur.

The question remains: Will the state legislature bend to the will of the citizens or the will of the corporations? And what can be done at the county level to counteract whatever may happen at the state level? The Pittsylvania County supervisors have already proven they are not amenable. When they were asked by their constituents to enact a resolution requesting the legislature to maintain the temporary ban on uranium mining, they refused.

Organizing in Pittsylvania

Pittsylvania is a large county, 978 total square miles, with a population of 61,745. The county abounds in historic places and old mansions. Families here trace their roots back to the Revolutionary era. Chatham is the county seat. The town has two private schools, which are a major part of the economic engine for the community. The mayor, George Haley, concerned about uranium mining, called an exploratory meeting of some of the citizens in order to gather more information.

One of attendees at the meeting was Gregg Vickrey, who moved to the area with his wife and three children twelve years earlier after determining that this friendly town was where he wanted to settle his family forever. He had always felt an obligation to give back, so when the mayor asked him to get involved, he said yes and started to research uranium mining. As someone who would be living five miles from the actual blasting site, Vickrey had a personal stake to make sure the area remains safe for his family. He found so many of his fellow Chatham residents equally concerned that they decided to hold a seminar. They invited some of the members of Halifax Southside Concerned Citizens, and Virginia Uranium was also invited to present their side of the case. Two hundred and fifty people attended the seminar.

Virginia Uranium's presentation revolved around the need to expand the nuclear power industry. Vickrey and Shireen Parsons addressed the issue of uranium mining in the community. Then the audience had a lot of questions for the Virginia Uranium representatives about how they planned to prevent contamination from their open-pit uranium mines, none of which they seemed able to answer. Their default position was that the state government would tell them how to mine the ore and keep things safe. After the seminar, Vickrey realized that the community needed to be truly educated about the hazards of uranium mining and decided to develop his own presentation. He also formed the Pittsylvania branch of Southside Concerned Citizens, which has evolved into the Teaching Human Empowerment Alliance.

> GREGG VICKREY: This is more than a uranium-mining issue. It's really an issue dealing with people's rights.

Obstacles and Challenges

A lot of people in the community still believed their government would save them. Some were reassured by the fact that the study had been approved in the recent general assembly, ignoring that the state would pay for the study in tandem with developing regulation for mining, or that the study would be conducted with the financial support of the coal and nuclear industries. Also, as Vickrey pointed out, the state had yet to ask residents if they wanted mining in their community: "This just shows that our governing authorities are ruling instead of serving. It should be about the Virginia Coal and Energy Commission doing our will instead of the corporation's will."

Another challenge was that Virginia communities have no rights encoded in law. This means they don't have recourse to get an issue on a referendum or ballot as they would in a home-rule community. Instead, Southside citizens will have to stand up against their own supervisors, their state legislature, and perhaps even the federal government. To do so, they are busily spreading the word in new ways, and their organization is evolving.

Organizing in Mecklenburg County

After the Bannister River flows right by the mine site, it feeds into Kerr Lake, which lies in Mecklenburg County, adjacent to Halifax. Here is where Barry Carter, engineer and author, is building a sustainable community. Carter, a member of the Occoneechee band of the Saponi nation, is also part African American. His family has lived in Mecklenburg County for generations. Carter realizes that in order for his community to survive, it needs a livable planet, and he has become a skillful activist who credits the Internet for much of his success. In one particular alliance with various traditional environmental organizations, he successfully mobilized a huge network to fight a golf course that was to be constructed in the Occoneechee State Park.

> BARRY CARTER: We succeeded against the odds, because the information age shifts power to people by allowing us to bypass so-called authorities. I don't know if traditional organizing groups yet understand this power shift, which allows the re-emergence of tribal networking systems.

Carter was growing increasingly concerned about the threat of uranium mining. After attending a CELDF presentation and a one-day Democracy School, he decided to shift focus and put more effort into fighting off uranium mining throughout the state of Virginia. The core of the strategy is indeed self-governance, but Carter felt that, since uranium deposits are located throughout the state, information technology could be used to educate and empower citizens in every county. He sees the main obstacle as fear:

> We're being told we have to dig up uranium and poison the earth and ourselves in order to have energy and fill

our bellies for another day. But we don't. That's rampant fear making us crazy. We can manage without uranium.

Following a one-day Democracy School, Pittsylvania County citizens began a petition campaign to collect signatures in every district of the county, demanding that the board of supervisors enact a chemical trespass ordinance. They have already collected thousands of signatures, and they are trying to reach a majority of citizens, not just voters. Their intent is that the citizens of each county district will present their signatures to their particular supervisor, and then all the signatures will be presented to the county board. Vickrey comments:

> Basically, our intention is to take back our governing authority. Once we have 51 percent, the supervisors will be given a choice to pass the ordinance, based on the signatures. If they move to enact the ordinance, then we will work with them to create more laws that give more governing authority to citizens. If they don't, we'll go back to the same people who signed the petition and tell them that their supervisors don't care about them or about what they want, so here is next petition.

The next petition would build on the chemical trespass petition, adding a crucial demand: If the board of supervisors doesn't act, the people will nullify the board and form a government that will.

The Declaration of Independence is alive and well.

Petition of Pittsylvania County

We the People of Pittsylvania County, in order to secure local self-government, democracy, and protect the health, safety, and welfare of the residents and environment of Pittsylvania County, hereby demand:

That the Pittsylvania County Board of Supervisors adopt an Ordinance that bans uranium mining from occurring within the County, and that the Ordinance be adopted within three months of the submission of this Petition to the Board of Supervisors;

That local governments in Pittsylvania County adopt Ordinances that protect residents from uranium mining, as a disincentive for the mining to occur;

That if the Pittsylvania County Board of Supervisors fails to take action to ban the mining, the Board will have failed to represent the majority of the people within the County under Article 1, Paragraph 2 of the Virginia Constitution, which declares that "all power is vested in, and consequently derived from, the people";

That if the Pittsylvania County Board of Supervisors does not represent the majority of people in the County, that is has rendered itself illegitimate under the Virginia Constitution, and that Article 1, Paragraph 3 of the Virginia Constitution

provides that "a majority of the community hath an indubi-
table, inalienable, and indefeasible right to reform, alter, or
abolish it";

That the undersigned, representing a majority of the residents
of Pittsylvania County, hereby call for a vote of the residents
to elect eleven people to draft a Constitution for the County
of Pittsylvania that bans uranium mining while recognizing
the right to community self-government. The undersigned call
on the Pittsylvania County Chapter of Southside Concerned
Citizens to develop and implement a democratic voting process
for the election of those eleven individuals;

That the undersigned, representing a majority of the residents
of Pittsylvania County, hereby call for a vote of the residents
to ratify the finalized Constitution, and declare that the
County Supervisors be given the option to adopt the Constitution, and that if they fail to do so, that the County Constitution shall automatically become the new governing law of
the County. If the County Supervisors refuse to adopt the new
Constitution, the undersigned hereby authorize that another
vote be taken to elect new County Supervisors, who shall
possess the legal and constitutional mandate to replace the
existing County Supervisors.

Chapter 6

THE CALL

Approximately 350,000 people are now living under the new laws and frameworks described in this book. Instead of focusing their energy on fighting the structures of power in this country, these brave citizens are instead working to create the kinds of communities they want to live in, governed by a law they can believe in.

Other communities are taking up the struggle. Newfield and Shapleigh, Maine, recently voted in an ordinance giving rights to nature and banning Nestle Waters from withdrawing water resources. Nearby Wells Township is considering doing the same. In California, the community of Mount Shasta is in the process of passing an ordinance that would ban corporate cloud-seeding, while Nevada City is looking at a sustainable-watershed ordinance. Crestone, Colorado, has recently become interested in using a CELDF approach in response to mining threats. Some cities are beginning to show an interest in what Spokane is doing in amending its charter to include citizens' rights.

Looking to the future, the conflict over natural resources will only continue to be more pervasive on our crowded planet. Our governmental institutions are too slow in responding to the planetary crisis we humans find ourselves in.

Everyday citizens are taking up the call by creating smaller and more sustainable forms of interaction,

trade, and locally supported economies. Farmers' markets, co-ops, alternative energy companies, and social justice organizations are pioneering new models that will need new forms of law.

In each of the communities discussed in this book, new ordinances have stopped the immediate threat while directly challenging the legal authority of corporations to override community decision-making. Equally important, these ordinances are a tool for starting the broader and critical conversation about how our structure of law works, and for whom.

This conversation is the work of the Community Environmental Legal Defense Fund and the goal of the Democracy School, which is now taught in both longer and shorter versions, and is continually developing in tandem with the work on the ground level. As the demand for these schools grows, new teachers and organizers are training to expand the conversation. CELDF has now taught over 175 Democracy Schools in twenty-four states.

This movement would not be growing if so many communities weren't finding themselves in a test of will against a corporation, whether a factory farm, a quarry, a mining operation, or a water-withdrawal plant. However, over the years, CELDF organizers have shifted away from a focus on fighting corporations themselves to the process of defining and ensuring the rights of the people.

Powerful as they are, and destructive as they can be, corporate entities maintain their entitlement in some part because citizens doubt that they can govern themselves.

Traditional environmental organizations have not proven themselves allied to the approach that CELDF advocates, as it calls into question some of their assumptions and accomplishments, as well as their position of expertise and privilege. And, for the same reason, environmental and other lawyers, embedded as they are within settled law, often line up against CELDF's work.

Pennsylvania Pushback

It's important for activists to remember that opposition from corporations and government is not a failure of organizing but a necessary stage of its expression. Opposition makes the stakes clear to people who may still harbor the illusion of safety and control.

CELDF got started in Pennsylvania, where many communities have passed ordinances banning toxic sludge dumping, corporate farming, quarries, incinerators, and longwall coal mining. The powers that be have not taken kindly to this assertion of self-governance by local communities. House Bill 1646 has been introduced and signed into law, which empowers the Pennsylvania attorney general to sue local municipalities to overturn ordinances.

Citizens have come to realize that if they want to be able to control what goes on in their homes and communities, they will have to follow in the footsteps of the abolitionists and the suffragists, who focused on changing the very law of the land.

Changing settled law is not a short-term project. While building a movement, local laws will be challenged by corporations and the state and federal governments that wield them. This is occurring now in a number of ways. The supervisors of Packer Township, Pennsylvania, assume they will face lawsuits and are preparing their citizens for this eventuality. Over in west Pennsylvania, two coal corporations have filed a lawsuit contending that the anti-corporate mining ordinance adopted by the Blaine Township supervisors violates the corporations' constitutional rights under the First, Fourth, Fifth, and Fourteenth Amendments of the United States Constitution, as well rights guaranteed by the constitution's Commerce and Contracts Clause. The coal corporations also contend that the ordinance is preempted by Pennsylvania state mining laws. They demand that a federal court nullify the ordinance. The Blaine supervisors are 100 percent in line to defend their new laws. They have held a public meeting and invited the community in to review the lawsuit, to ask questions, to discuss liability, and to once again make it clear what their rationale is for standing up to the coal corporations. With the help of CEDLF, the Blaine supervisors have filed a motion to dismiss the coal corporations' claims, contending that the corporations lack any constitutional rights within the township, and therefore have no constitutional rights that can be violated. Appeals to higher courts are expected, and this case and others will test how our present laws will be interpreted to favor either corporate power or citizens' rights.

Thomas Linzey and Ben Price, the local CELDF organizer on the ground in Pennsylvania, continue to work with Michael Vacca and the Buffalo Creek group. They are mounting a campaign to change Blaine from a municipal second-class township to a home-rule municipality.

As communities turn to the courts to change settled law, they start to recognize that this process may take many, many years. And legislatures will not change the law as long as they are beholden to companies fighting to squeeze their profits from the earth's dwindling resources. CELDF is therefore engaged in examining what other mechanisms will get communities what they want—a right to self-governance driven into the framework of law. In Pennsylvania, CELDF has created a document for townships to sign, asking for a Pennsylvania Constitutional Convention to be convened in order to create a new state constitution guaranteeing the right to local self-government and protecting the rights of residents and communities.

The Rights of Nature Gain Traction

Tamaqua Borough was the first community to give nature a right to exist. Since that time, communities in Pennsylvania, New Hampshire, and Virginia have adopted new laws that change the status of natural communities and ecosystems from being regarded as property under the law to being recognized as rights-bearing entities. These laws recognize that natural communities and ecosystems possess a fundamental right to exist and to flourish, and that residents of these communities possess the legal authority to enforce those rights on behalf of the ecosystem.

Ecuador's New Constitution

Recently, an international nonprofit organization that supports indigenous people in the Amazon in claiming stewardship over local rainforests learned of Thomas Linzey's work and asked him for assistance. The driving concern of the Pachamama Alliance was to give the indigenous people of Ecuador the rights that have been denied to native tribes throughout the Americas, rights that would in turn empower the tribes to protect their natural environment and rainforests. It turned out that the country was engaged in a rewrite of its constitution and rethinking some fundamental principles.

In Montechristi, a tiny town on the Ecuadoran coast, Linzey and CELDF associate Mari Margil presented rights-of-nature concepts to different committees and wound up meeting with the president of the Ecuador Constitutional Assembly. Not long after that meeting, the assembly voted to adopt these fundamental rights. The new constitution was approved by an overwhelming margin through a national referendum vote. With that vote, Ecuador became the first country in the world to codify a new system of environmental protection based on the rights of nature—an exceptional event that gives hope to people struggling all over the world. Hopefully this will lead the way for other countries, including our own, to make the necessary and fundamental constitutional change in how we protect nature.

Additions to the Ecuador Constitution

Article 1. Nature or Pachamama, where life is reproduced and exists, has the right to exist, persist, maintain itself and regenerate its own vital cycles, structure, functions, and its evolutionary processes.

Any person, people, community, or nationality, may demand the observance of the rights of the natural environment before public bodies. The application and interpretation of these rights will follow the related principles established in the Constitution.

Article 2. Nature has the right to be completely restored. This complete restoration is independent of the obligation on natural and juridical persons or the State to compensate people or collective groups that depend on the natural systems.

In the cases of severe or permanent environmental impact, including the ones caused by the exploitation of nonrenewable natural resources, the State will establish the most efficient mechanisms for the restoration, and will adopt the adequate measures to eliminate or mitigate the harmful environmental consequences.

Article 3. The State will motivate natural and juridical persons as well as collectives to protect nature; it will promote respect towards all the elements that form an ecosystem.

Article 4. The State will apply precaution and restriction measures in all the activities that can lead to the extinction of species, the destruction of the ecosystems, or the permanent alteration of the natural cycles.

The introduction of organisms and organic and inorganic material that can alter in a definitive way the national genetic heritage is prohibited.

Article 5. The persons, people, communities, and nationalities will have the right to benefit from the environment and form natural wealth that will allow well-being.

Where to Start

ADDITIONAL INFORMATION
FOR READERS AND ACTIVISTS
INTERESTED IN CREATING
LASTING CHANGE IN THEIR
OWN COMMUNITIES

Assess the issues at hand.

What is the issue that you and your community are facing? Are there immediate threats? Are there battles that have been fought over and over? Collect data. Talk to people in the community who have evidence and experience with the problem. What remedies have been tried and failed? Use the Internet or go to your public library to gather more information. Are people open to a new approach? On what issue can you get a committed group of people to push for change?

Contact the Community Environmental Legal Defense Fund about teaching Democracy School in your area.

CELDF currently teaches Democracy School in both a three-day and a one-day format. Visit www.celdf.org to review information on how to help your community start down the path toward self-governance. E-mail or call to find out if there is a particular organizer in your area.

If no school is available in your area, you can still engage in the conversation, using CELDF materials. Ask: Who decides what happens in our communities right now? What kind of relationship do we want to have with each other, with nature? What rights do we want to encode in law? The use of media, such as documentary films, helps a great deal in spreading information and inspiration. As much as possible, research the history of corporate power and rights so you know what your community is up against.

There are also videos available on the CELDF Web site that show how each of the communities described in this book went about their organizing. These can be used to inspire your own community.

Encourage participation.

Encourage everyone you contact to attend local meetings and/or the Democracy School. After your core group defines its vision, it's time to set goals, such as passing an ordinance or similar action that reclaims sovereignty in your community.

Deepen bonds and form alliances.

Creating real change takes time, so keep the enthusiasm alive. Schedule meetings and conversations. Have house parties, potluck dinners—whatever it takes to spread the word and stay focused. Continue building relationships: each person brings particular skills, and it's important to appreciate individual talents and interests. A good rapport will help your group through the difficult times ahead.

Talk to other community groups; many are dealing with the same underlying issue but feel isolated. You may find allies in places you don't suspect, such as your church, your PTA, neighbors, or civil rights groups. Talk to leaders in your area—not just elected leaders, but also the local clergy, social and environmental justice groups, various clubs, and the chamber of commerce. Forming alliances is essential to getting results.

Resources

Community Environmental Legal Defense Fund

675 Mower Road

Chambersburg, Pennsylvania 17202

info@celdf.org

www.celdf.org | 717.709.0457

Advocates for Community Empowerment

382 Old Walpole Road

Keene, New Hampshire 03431

Ellen Hayes: 603.252.1411

ellen@acene.org

Bioneers

A New Mexico-based nonprofit organization promoting practical and innovative solutions to environmental and social problems. Bioneers holds an annual conference each October in San Rafael, California, and its plenary sessions are broadcast through satellite feeds to "Beaming Bioneers" conferences held simultaneously at sites in various locations throughout the United States and Canada. www.bioneers.org

Buffalo Creek Conservation Association

40 First Street, Taylorstown, Pennsylvania 13657

Michael Vacca: 724.948.3887

Fred Cramer: 724.948.3654

Citizens of Barnstead for a Living Democracy

180 Shackford Corner Road

Center Barnstead, New Hampshire 03225

Gail Darrell: geodarrell@yahoo.com

Corman Cullinan

Wild Law: Protecting Biological and Cultural Diversity

www.100Fires.com

Envision Spokane

2816 West Broadway

Spokane, Washington 99201

www.envisionspokane.org | 509.328.1475

Thom Hartmann

Author of *Cracking the Code: How to Win Hearts, Change Minds, and Restore America's Original Vision; Unequal Protection: The Rise of Corporate Dominance and the Theft of Human Rights; What Would Jefferson Do? A Return to Democracy;* and *We the People: A Call to Take Back America.*

The Thom Hartmann Radio Program is broadcast live daily from noon to 3:00 p.m. Eastern Time in Chicago, Detroit, Grand Rapids, Los Angeles, Memphis, Minneapolis, Phoenix, Pittsburgh, Portland, San Francisco, Santa Barbara, Seattle, and over fifty other radio stations nationwide, and on XM and Sirius Satellite radio.

www.thomhartmann.com | 1.866.987.THOM (8466)

Institute for Local Self-Reliance
www.ilsr.org/index.html

Nottingham Tea Party
Gail and Chris Mills: 603.942.8969
millscg@gmail.com

Pachamama Alliance
Dedicated to protecting the Earth's rain forests and the indigenous peoples who live within them.
www.pachamama.org

Program on Corporations, Law & Democracy (POCLAD)
A group of people instigating conversations and actions to contest the authority of corporations to define our culture, govern our nation, and plunder the Earth.
www.poclad.org | people@poclad.org

Subsided Ground, Fallen Futures

A documentary film about longwall coal mining. Written and directed by Terri Taylor. Produced by the Raymond Profitt Foundation.

www.rayprofitt.org

Sustainable Communities Network

www.sustainable.org

Tamaqua Borough, Pennsylvania

Cathy Miorelli: mior1599@yahoo.com

570.668.1599

Joe Murphy: jmmurph@ptd.net

The Teaching Human Empowerment Alliance

Gregg Vickrey

232 North Main Street

Chatham, Virginia 24531

alliance123@yahoo.com

The Alliance123.blogspot.com

Thirst

A documentary film about water-resource management and community responses. By Alan Snitow and Deborah Kaufman.

www.pbs.org/pov/thirst